HOW THE PROS PLAY FOOTBALL

by Berry Stainback

Illustrated by Ed Vebell

Random House · New York

In memory of
Jack Zanger,
who wrote about football
as he wrote about
all things,
with affection...
and then left
too soon

CONTENTS

Introduction

The more one watches football games over the years, the more questions the game raises. You sit in the stands or in front of a television set and you wonder. How did that free safety know to leave the halfback he was covering and race over to help the strongside cornerback defend against a pass—in time to intercept the ball? How did the center tie up that big middle linebacker before he could get to the back carrying off tackle? How did the quarterback read that zone defense quickly enough to complete a pass right between two defense backs? What are the keys a player must read to react so precisely to his responsibility and put him in the right place at the right time?

It was decided that the best way to find out the answers was to ask the players themselves. We chose 16 All-Star performers covering every position in the game and asked them to talk about their jobs. We weren't interested in personality or characterization —although obviously these would emerge in the way the players described their techniques and the way they applied them. We were interested in insights, in taking the sophisticated fan and the youngster who wanted to improve his play right inside the heads of top pros as they prepared for and performed in ballgames. Many of them sat down with us right after practice in their dressing cubicles. Others talked while relaxing in their homes on a Monday—traditionally the players' only "off" day during the season. Still others answered questions in hotel rooms on Saturday afternoons before road games.

We want to thank the 16 players who took the time to so thoroughly describe their jobs. Thanks, too, to the National Football League Players Association for its cooperation, particularly to President John Mackey and to Mal Kennedy, the director of business affairs, who aided this project whenever he was called upon right from the start.   B.S.

Defensive

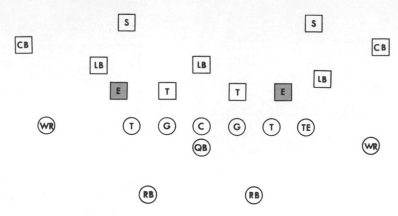

CARL ELLER
Defensive End

Most pro football experts say it takes six or seven years for a defensive player to become a truly outstanding all-round performer. Bob Hollway of the Minnesota Vikings, who coaches perhaps the best all-round rush line in pro football, says, "Your front four players don't get great until the 28-year-old range. These boys have big bodies, and it seems to take a while for their coordination to catch up, for them to put the whole game together."

Defensive end Carl Eller, the Vikings' number one draft choice in 1964, put his whole game together at age 25. That was in 1967 when Eller was named to the first-team All-Pro squad by the three major selectors: AP, UPI and NEA.

"It takes a few years for a defensive lineman to mature, to adjust," Eller admits. "It's a question of mental judgment and experience. Sometimes in the early years you . . ." he pauses, smiling, "miscalculate. But then you get to know your opponents, the offensive tackles and quarterbacks. You might still have mental lapses, sure, but your experience will make the difference and you can recover. That's what will give you stature, that consistency—not just on one play but through the whole game."

Never was Eller's consistency more apparent than in back-to-back games with the Green Bay Packers and Detroit

Lions. The games were played toward the end of the 1968 season, when the Vikings were going for their first division title. Eller spent both Sundays in the opponents' offensive backfields and earned himself matching game balls. Against the Packers he made two particularly crucial tackles. The first came on a big third-down play when halfback Donny Anderson ran a sweep around the opposite end from Eller. But Carl charged in so fast that he ran Anderson down from behind before the halfback could turn the corner. On a subsequent third-down-and-long-yardage situation, Eller hit Forrest Gregg so hard that the veteran All-league offensive tackle's helmet sailed off his head. Carl sailed right past him and banged into quarterback Bart Starr with such force that he had to be helped off the field. Starr returned shortly thereafter, but began calling plays that made no sense at all. He was escorted to the sideline for good to clear his groggy head. That was the third time Eller had sacked Starr by himself during the afternoon. In addition, Carl went in at tight end and blocked for what proved to be the winning touchdown, and he also blocked a Packer field-goal attempt.

In the Lion game, the entire Viking front four camped in the opposing backfield. They forced Detroit into fumbling ten times, an NFL record, and dropped quarterback Bill Munson for losses four times. Eller alone tackled Munson twice and was singled out as the top defensive player in the game.

To hear Eller tell it, what he does on a football field isn't so great. "The basic responsibilities of my job are to rush the passer and to stop the running plays that come to my side. More specifically, to stop any running plays through the five hole [between guard and tackle], through the seven hole [between tackle and end] and any plays that are outside me. That's all there is to it.

"Holes" in the offensive line (strong side).

"Now, there are two different styles used in trying to get to the quarterback. One is the 'elusive' style and the other is the 'attacking' style. The elusive is where you would be trying to avoid the offensive tackle, keeping him away from you as much as possible while still getting to the quarterback. This requires a lot of faking and quickness to get the tackle going one way while you go the other before he gets set. The other style, the attacking, is where you would be trying to attack the offensive tackle, trying to throw him aside to beat him in your pursuit of the quarterback.

"You generally end up using variations of these styles because one doesn't work all the time. You have to keep changing-up, using one and then the other. So characterizing the style of any defensive end would depend on how much he emphasizes one particular method. In other words, whether he is more elusive or more attacking. My style is more the attacking type, for example, and Deacon Jones of the Rams probably uses more of an elusive style most of the time."

Eller says the basic physical requirements of the defensive end are the same all along the line: "Size, strength, stamina, speed and quickness. Most defensive ends weigh between 240 and 265 pounds, with the average right around 250." That's Eller's weight nowadays. He has taken off some 14 pounds from his early playing weight. The loss of weight didn't affect his strength, and it did improve his quickness. As for pure speed, Carl is the fastest of the Viking front four. He has been timed at 4.5 seconds for 40 yards, which is faster than many backs, and he once caught Gale Sayers 20 yards downfield.

Two other physical assets that are invaluable to a pass rusher are height and reach. Eller stands six feet, six inches tall and has a 42-inch reach. If he penetrates an opponent's backfield even a couple of yards and throws his hands up, it is very difficult for a quarterback to keep his receivers in view. Even if the quarterback succeeds, he has to throw around that ten-foot wall (named Eller) that is moving in on him. No quarterback can throw over Eller once he's taken a couple of steps into the backfield. Since most of Carl's rushes are made from the outside, the quarterback must release the ball very quickly to complete short passes to Eller's side.

The physical requirements needed to play defensive end

5

come with the man, but the mental requirements have to be learned and take a little longer. Eller had such an exceptional rookie season in 1964 that Norm Van Brocklin, then the Viking coach, predicted Carl would be an All-Pro in no time. "Eller is so natural that things come easy to him," said Van Brocklin.

Carl *was* a natural; he had an unusually instinctive feel for playing defensive end. Yet for the most part it was his overwhelming physical attributes that got him through that first season in such fine fashion. The next two seasons he spent acquiring what he calls "the mental knowledge" of playing his position.

"The mental knowledge is a thorough knowledge of your opponent," Eller says. "Being able to study your opponent very carefully, being able to know what things to look for and being able to know what things they might use against you. You should have a great mental awareness of your own capabilities, too. That's very important. You have to know what your weak points are, because automatically a team or an individual opponent is going to try to hit you at those weak points. They're going to try to take advantage of them. Once you realize what your weak points are, you have to work to eliminate them. At the same time you also have to work to try to make your strong points stronger. You have to keep working to improve.

"Mentally, I think you have to concentrate totally on the game. I think this is the way to prepare yourself for a game—to keep yourself mentally alert, try to find out everything you can about your opponent and shut everything else out of your mind. The game takes priority over anything else that might come about. You have to make whatever sacrifice is necessary to win football games. Football is my everything. I've got no time for anything else during the season. It's hard for anything to interfere. The world could end, I guess, and I'd still be playing. Playing and working to do better."

An All-America defensive tackle at his high school in

Winston-Salem, North Carolina, Eller was named to some college All-America teams in his junior year at the University of Minnesota. As a senior he was a unanimous All-America selection and was the first man picked in the pro draft.

"The transition from tackle to end wasn't nearly as demanding as the transition from college to professional football," says Carl. "In both high school and college you're more adapted to defending against a running type of game, whereas in the pros it is more of a passing game."

Now that he is more experienced at it, Eller is particularly tough to run against. "The easiest play for me to execute is probably a straight-ahead running play," he says. "The thing that makes straight-ahead plays easy is that you can read them quickly and react right away. Also, the frequency of seeing them makes them easier. Of course, there have been instances when I haven't made this play. At times it can be more difficult than others. For instance, when it's a third-and-long situation and you're rushing hard expecting a pass, you can be in trouble if they run a play that hits quick. Or when I'm lined up farther outside than I would normally be, it's harder to get back inside to react to a running play that hits real quick.

"I remember the Green Bay game this season. It was a passing situation, I thought, third-and-seven or third-and-eight, something like that. I rushed hard and then the play hit very quick with Travis Williams carrying the ball. You know how fast he is and how quick he hits a hole. Well, by the time I saw that he was carrying, I had taken myself out of the play. Fortunately for us, Williams fell or tripped. Otherwise, he would have been carrying the ball a long way."

As with most defensive linemen, the toughest play for Eller to execute is the play-action pass. This, of course, is why quarterbacks are using it more and more in order to delay the pass rush for a second or so. The quarterback fakes a handoff to a running back going through the line, and the offensive lineman makes an initial block as if for a running play. But then the quarterback, who has shoved the ball toward the runner and then pulled it back, is fading to pass. The linemen have to read run first, but they have to pick up the fake very swiftly if they are to mount any kind of an effective pass rush at all—particularly on a short throw.

"When those linemen fire out at you as if it's a running play and then you find it's a pass, it's really difficult to get a good pass rush," Eller says, shaking his head. "Occasionally you can do it. Like in the last Pittsburgh game. When I got the quarterback the first time that he tried to throw the ball, it was on a play-pass action. I think I went to charge inside and the tackle went down with me to hit me low. I could see that the quarterback still had the ball and the backs were gone as he followed through on his play-pass fake. But then I was able to continue my pass rush without being held up on the line for too long.

"This is what you have to try to avoid—getting held up too long on the line reading run when it's a pass. Yet you've still got to react to the blocking that is coming at you . . . and when it's coming at you it indicates run. So you've got to handle it and keep looking in at the quarterback to see if he's hiding that ball on his hip or whatever. As soon as you check it out, then you continue your pass rush. If you check it out quick enough, you've got a shot at the quarterback; but even if you read the pass late, you've got to complete your maximum effort on the rush."

A rush lineman never knows when the quarterback might have to hold the ball an extra second, waiting for a receiver to get open. An end like Eller has got to keep pressing in to force the passer to unload as soon as possible. Obviously there are times when the fake is so well executed that the end—the entire rush line—is chasing a ball carrier who does not have the ball.

"I've had my share of those, too," Carl says. "When we were playing Detroit, Greg Landry pulled off a beautiful play-pass action. He sent both of his backs into the line and he hid the ball very well. I thought a back had the ball because I couldn't see the actual action, and the block that the offensive tackle used on me indicated run action—at least more so than pass. So I went down the line in pursuit, chasing the backs. Then I looked up and Landry was standing back there with the ball. He was throwing the long pass downfield for a completion. You can see how much time he had to get off a long one."

Only a few years ago many teams had two rushers on their front four and two other linemen who assumed a run first on every play. In other words, two men went in virtually flat-out on a pass rush on every play, while the other two defenders covered for the run before committing themselves to a rush. But pro football has gotten tougher and tougher over the years. Now all the good defenses require that their entire front fours cover their area after a first-step penetration before going after the quarterback. Offensive lines have gotten stronger as a unit, and they are quick to take advantage of overaggressive rush men, letting them take themselves right out of plays with their ferocity. Then a running back can zip through a big hole.

"I think Bob Brown of the Rams is the best offensive tackle in the League—the best I've faced," says Eller. "He's very big and very strong and he has good balance, *very good balance* for a man who weighs over 280 pounds. Yet he's also got quickness. So you take an offensive tackle who's got everything and, on top of that, is bigger than you, and you can see how difficult the job can be."

For all the difficulty of the job and all the frustrations that an end like Eller is subject to (especially since he is double-teamed much of the time), Carl has a strict rule about keeping his emotions under control. Even when he is consistently held, he never seems to lose his temper.

"I never get angry at an opponent," he says. "He's doing his job and he's trying to keep me from doing mine. That's all there is to it. Anger doesn't really make you play a better game. And that's what you're always striving to do—play a better game."

9

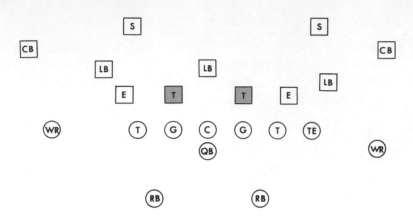

BOB LILLY
Defensive Tackle

Bob Lilly of the Dallas Cowboys has been the best defensive tackle in the National Football League for years. Not long ago he was talking about the requirements needed to play the position. "First of all," he said, "you have to be pretty big. I'm six feet, five inches and weigh 255 pounds, yet I'm the shortest man on our rush line. You also have to be pretty quick to be a good defensive tackle. You've got to get off the ball fast. You have to be able to think fast, too—recognize what the offense is doing right away. And it's reached the point now where you've got to be half mean. You have to feel that every time you get a chance to take a shot at somebody, you have to take it. That's not the way I am personally, but that's the way I have to be to do my job properly."

Guards around the League are thankful that Lilly isn't actually a mean football player. He is so quick and so strong that it is literally impossible for any one man to block him consistently. For example, in 1964 Lilly emerged as a top tackle. At the season's end, when the Cowboy coaching staff studied the game films to check out the performance of each of their players, they found that Lilly had broken the first block on him *every single time* throughout the season. Against that kind of player, what's a guard to do? The answer is—hold. Grab Lilly's jersey and hang on for your quarterback's dear life.

Lilly is not one to complain if the officials don't call the infraction. But his silence encourages guards to try an even tighter grip.

The strongest comment Bob has ever made on the subject is: "I don't mind being held. But when they start tearing my jersey off my shoulder pads, then it's bad. It's part of the game, though. I've just got to overcome the holding myself." That's why he says he has to be mean. "When a man's holding you, you've got to start beating him in the head."

Bob Lilly just isn't the type to do this very often, but perhaps he'll change eventually. His whole philosophy of playing defensive tackle has changed over the years. He was always taught to play the run first and then the pass. But in their early seasons the Cowboys lost so many games because of long passes that Lilly concentrated more on rushing the passer than on reading the running plays. He had so much speed that he would burst all the way in on a quarterback, only to find that he had handed off on a draw play. Then Lilly would turn and run down the back who was carrying the ball. The back might pick up a few yards, of course, but at least a receiver hadn't caught a touchdown pass.

As soon as the Cowboys' secondary improved, Lilly began following coach Tom Landry's philosophy more closely. "I understand what he's talking about now," says Lilly. "You can play the pass okay, but the first thing you have to do is play the run. Stop that and you force them into a passing situation. Then you can rush all out. To play the run you have to be strong. You have to be able to hold your position and stop them in the middle of the line. You also have to have good pursuit. Except for the middle linebacker, the tackles are in the best position to get into good pursuit.

"On the Cowboys we play a very coordinated type of defense. Everybody has a place to be, an area to cover when the ball is snapped. A lot of times this gives us a little slower pass rush than some other teams—say, for instance, the Rams, who just blow in. They're probably coordinated to an extent, too, but they're going a lot harder on the snap of the ball. There are different ways to play the position, different styles of overall defense. Our philosophy is to play the position first, read the run, then rush the passer."

The defensive tackle keys on the center, the guard or the

tackle on his side. It depends on the area he's responsible for on the particular rush that's been called. In other words, Lilly sometimes works a deal with his end in which Lilly loops around to the outside and the end comes inside him. This, of course, changes the keys.

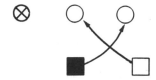

Tackle and defensive end "loop."

"Our first step is on the snap of the ball," says Bob. "This puts us in the slot where we're supposed to be. As soon as we get there we immediately recognize if it's a pass or a run and react accordingly. This is just recognition. We work on it all week. If it's a pass, we keep right on going in. This does slow you down a second. But the only way you can get hurt by it is if they manage to complete a lot of short passes. Your secondary is more vulnerable to the short pass this way. But we feel that even if they can short-pass nine or ten times, it's not going to work out well for them in the long run. Every time they put the ball in the air they take a chance on an interception. Or they're going to miss a few. The ball may bounce off a shoulder pad, or the receiver might drop the ball . . . Even if he catches it, a lot of times it's only for a two- or three-yard gain, so they haven't gained much. And we try to put enough pressure on the quarterback to make him throw quick."

The tackles, who rush inside, try to force the quarterback to drop back deep or move out of the pocket. In that way, the ends coming from the outside have a good shot at him. If the end gets in quicker, he will force the quarterback to step up—right into the arms of the onrushing tackle. Lilly and his tackle partner on the Cowboys, six-foot, six-inch Jethro Pugh, try to break their blocks on the inside. They drive in hard, then raise their hands up high to shield the passer's view or at least distract him from the receiver.

"I've got about four moves I work on all the time in rushing the passer," says Bob, who plays right tackle. "On one I'll make a quick drive into the center-guard gap, duck my left shoulder, and raise my right arm up. If I'm getting off the ball quick enough, I'll be by the guard before he knows what's happening. Another thing I do is grab the guard by the jersey and take an inside step (toward the center). If he comes with me, I'll throw him on in and rush outside. A third move I make is an arm swipe. That's where you hit the opposing man's helmet with your hand and try to knock him off balance. Then you go by him to the other side. Still another thing I do is grab the guard's jersey and butt him in the head with my helmet. While he's trying to recover, I release him with one arm and throw the other arm over his shoulder to get my elbow back there. Whichever side I'm going to, I've got my elbow over there to push myself by him."

Lilly, of course, is so good that no guard is expected to handle him without help. Every time Bob beats the guard to the inside, the center picks him up. That makes it extremely difficult for the All-league tackle to reach the quarterback since he has only three seconds. What he hopes to do is penetrate enough to drive the quarterback deeper—to where the end can get him. On his outside rushes Lilly has a better shot, even on a double-team, because a running back usually picks him up.

"Then I do something different," says Bob. "The back is coiled, ready to fire at you. You rush right up to him and the instant you get there, you take a fake step to the side and go right on around him. He'll usually fire out and miss. Or sometimes you can even jump right over the back if he fires at you too soon."

Except for a year or so as a defensive end with the Cowboys, Bob Lilly has been a defensive tackle ever since his senior year in high school in Throckmorton, Texas. Football, of course, is king in Texas and Bob learned solid fundamentals right from the start.

"Tackle in high school and college is not the same as in pro football," he says, "though it's similar. In both places you're in the middle of all the action. There's always somebody hitting you. Of course, if you're getting hit, then you know you're doing your job as far as pursuit goes. If they're worried about your pursuit, they're going to have somebody hitting you all the time. I like it in the middle. You've got to think pretty fast in there, and you're in the game all the time."

Lilly's pursuit is so strong that, in the early years of his pro career, opponents took advantage of it. They would use influence blocks to get him pursuing one way, then come right back through the hole he had left. For example, they would pull his guard to the strong side and Bob would chase after him—while the back ran through Lilly's weak-side tackle spot. When Bob saw what they were doing to him, he began sitting a little longer in order to get a more accurate reading before pursuing.

Opponents no longer try to use influence blocks on him. When Lilly stopped chasing the guard, the poor ball carrier would have to run right into the unblocked Lilly. This hurt. Now the only thing opponents can do to minimize Lilly's pursuit is to run right at him. But he's so strong that he tends to toss away the blockers and drop the runner himself. (When he was at Texas A&M he used to pick up Volkswagens for laughs.)

"The toughest thing for me now is the play-action pass," says Bob. "As I said, we read the run first. Naturally, when the play looks like a run we react to stopping a ball carrier. Then, when it turns out we're wrong, we have to come off that and go for the passer. It's tough for me, or for anyone else who plays with a system like ours. I'm getting to recognize the play-action better all the time, though. I remember when the Giants worked it on us about twenty times a few years ago. Fran Tarkenton would roll as if it was a run. I would pursue along the line and the center would block down on me. The next thing I knew they'd completed a pass. Greg Larson [the Giant center] does a great job of blocking on these play-action passes.

"Well, in our last game against the Giants, Tarkenton rolled as if it was a run and Larson came over on me. It was the only time during the game that he tried the choke block, but I just instinctively recognized the pass. Which I should after he's worked it about twenty times." Bob laughed. "Anyway, I took off and got by Larson real fast and I got Fran. I nearly got him for a safety. It was just recognition. Like I said, after twenty times I ought to recognize it. And I had a little more freedom in that particular situation down near the goal line and I just got off the ball real well."

When he was playing more of a free-lance style of tackle, Lilly used to have trouble with the draw plays. In fact, he had trouble on any delayed hand-offs that took place after he had passed them in an effort to get to the quarterback.

"Even after our first four or five years here," says Bob, "we wanted to get the passer so badly that we'd just take off. We weren't coordinated in our pass rush or anything. So we used to worry about the draws. Now, if the draw play is coming my way, I recognize it almost instantaneously. I don't necessarily make the play, but I make the back go through another hole. When you do that, of course, somebody is going to get him because all the blocking's been thrown off. The Giants ran two or three in that last game, but I didn't make any tackles because they were all run to the other side.

"Of course, you can still miss them when they're to your side. In our last game against Philadelphia I charged in. I even had my arms around the waist of the ball carrier who was running the draw. But I was running so fast on the rush that he pulled away from me and made three or four yards. That's when they get by you—when you blow in there for the pass. It happened on a third-and-long play and I just blew in there. But it worked out because they didn't get a first down.

"A lot of guys will stop when they recognize the draw coming. But that's the worst thing you can do. All the blocker has to do then is just bump you. When I recognize the draw coming, I try to move that much faster. I think that's the best thing you can do once you've committed yourself. Get in there as quick as you can and try to mess up the play."

Ironically, Lilly will beat some of the most highly respected guards in the league without seeming to work up a sweat. And then he will seem to have all kinds of trouble with an unknown guard. One reason he can get past the stars so easily is that their techniques are opposite. The only reason he has trouble with a rookie is that he doesn't get "up" for him.

"A defensive lineman who's going against a rookie tends not to regard him real highly," Lilly admits. "I remember this guy I was playing against in Pittsburgh. Well, even though he looked pretty good in the films, I just didn't pay much attention to him. Then when we played Pittsburgh, I guarantee you he just ate my lunch. I didn't even get close to the quarterback.

"There was also a guard in San Francisco, a second-year man. Well, I didn't take him very seriously either. But after playing against him a few times and not getting the quarterback—not even getting near the quarterback—well, I kind of got respect for him."

Of course, even so, some of Lilly's greatest days have come against young guards. For instance, he went against a second-year man in Pittsburgh some years ago, and the poor fellow hasn't recovered to this day.

"I think our whole defensive line had a great surge in that particular game," says Bob. "For some reason our whole line was at a peak, and the Steelers just couldn't concentrate on anybody. We dropped the quarterback thirteen times in that game, and I think I got in there about five times. It was great. Any defensive lineman will tell you that getting to the quarterback is the thing. You can stop the run and everything else but, boy, I'll tell you—when you get to the quarterback, that's the game! 'Cause he's the guy you're after. When you get him, it's the greatest satisfaction."

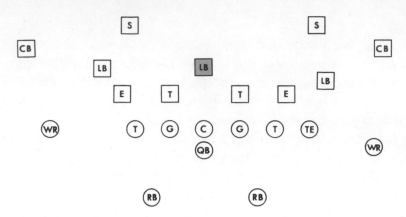

DICK BUTKUS
Middle Linebacker

"There are different ways to play middle linebacker," says Dick Butkus, a 6-foot-3, 245-pounder who plays for the Chicago Bears. "I figure I'm probably one of the biggest, or heaviest, men at the position in the National League, so I think I can handle the runs real well, and I can still handle the passes fairly well, too."

Some teams are going with lighter, faster middle linebackers these days in an effort to strengthen their defense against the pass. Leroy Jordan of the Dallas Cowboys weighs only 215 pounds, for example. Butkus doesn't feel this lighter, quicker trend makes sense.

"It's impossible to find a person who's big enough to handle the run and still keep up with a Gale Sayers or a Leroy Kelly on pass coverages for any distance," Dick says. "What I think is that a middle linebacker should be anywhere from 230 to 250 pounds, but he's got to have a lot of agility. He doesn't necessarily have to have pure speed—a 9.9 man in the 100-yard dash, for instance. But he does have to have a lot of agility, be able to move well laterally and take on a 250-pound center who's coming out to block him, get rid of that center and go over and make the tackle or help out on the tackle. Yet he's also got to be able to keep up with a halfback or fullback on a pass to a certain extent.

18

"I know people say that that's one of my weaknesses—that I don't have enough speed to keep up with a halfback. Well, I don't think there's *any* middle linebacker—or any linebacker at all—who can keep up with an offensive back who goes deep for a pass. So I think that criticism is a bunch of baloney. Because you very seldom get caught. Very seldom does the quarterback have enough time to throw a deep pass to someone who's in a one-on-one situation with a linebacker.

"The rush line continually puts pressure on the quarterback, and the good middle linebacker reads the pass quickly enough to be able to get back into his coverage with a good jump on the offensive back. After all, the back starts three yards deep in his backfield, and the middle linebacker is usually a yard or so behind the line of scrimmage. Then, too, the middle linebacker often has help down the deep middle from the free safety, who is back farther, moves faster and is also reading the play.

"So I'd go with a middle linebacker who has real good agility and a keen sense for the ball," says Butkus. This instinct for the ball—a sort of innate feel for where it is and what's going to develop—is probably the most crucial asset a middle linebacker can have beyond his physical skills. As Butkus says, "You've got to have a nose for the ball and be able to react to it right *now*. If it's a handoff in the backfield, the middle linebacker has to know immediately: Is it going to be an off-tackle play? Is it coming up the middle? Is it a sweep—or is it a *fake* handoff and a pass? You've got to have a little sense for the ball and a little football knowledge in order to be able to react quickly enough to get into the play.

"And if it's a run you've got to be able to handle any type of lineman," Dick says, "because *all* offensive linemen get a shot at the middle linebacker—center, guards, tackles, tight end. It all depends on what running play it is. If it's a sweep, you have a 260- or 270-pound tackle coming at you. If it's a straightaway run, you have a 250-pound center or guard coming at you."

19

The middle linebacker's responsibilities vary with the defense that has been called for a particular play. The Bears use mainly a gap system in which the rush line and the linebackers are responsible for filling certain gaps that stretch from sideline to sideline. On pass defense, the secondary and linebackers are responsible for covering certain zones. The middle backer, depending on the defense, covers either of the three short zones—over the middle and to either flat. Generally, the middle backer has to handle running plays from the center out to either tackle. Often he is the tackler on sweeps, which the outside linebacker and the forcing defensive back contain while he comes up from the inside.

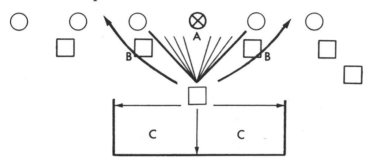

Middle linebacker's responsibilities:
a. Cover inside runs
b. Cover sweeps
c. Cover a short pass zone.

"On the run I've got to get rid of the man blocking me and cover my gap," Butkus says. "If I read that it's a passing play, I have to drop back into my zone right away. We have various zones, and we determine which ones we use by the formation the offense shows us. Now, if we're in a man-to-man defense, I have to look up my man and go cover him until he gets out of my zone. So your basic responsibilities are to do your job first, and then help out second."

Coming from a vocational high school in Chicago, Butkus was understandably not a scholar at the University of Illinois. But the charge that he was unintelligent was proved ridiculous when he joined the Bears in 1965 and called all the team's defenses. The Bears' owner, George Halas, would never have entrusted a dope with so much responsibility. Butkus called defenses up until the 1969 season when head coach Jim Dooley decided that calling them from the bench would give the team a little more advantage. The bench receives instant information on what opponents are doing from scouts high in the stands and is therefore in a better position to make judgments. But the Bears still rely on Butkus' football knowledge to call audibles that change the defense on the field.

"When they come out in a formation that the bench didn't anticipate for the particular defense they called," says Dick, "I'll call an audible at the line in order to change our whole defense. Say they come out in a formation that calls for man-to-man coverage and we've got a zone on—I'll audible it. So even though I don't call the defensive signals any more, I've still gotta know everything that we're gonna do and what kind of defense we're gonna run against every formation. I have to know what the opposition's strengths are, what they like to run on certain formations and in certain situations. What do they like to run on each of their formations on first and ten, or second and seven-plus, or second and five-minus? What do they like to use on short-yardage plays? What do they like to do down on the goal line? So you've got to be able to recognize the formation they come out in right away so that you can adjust your specific defense accordingly."

The Bears work all week studying their upcoming opponent so that they will have instant recognition of formations and know pretty much what to expect in the game. "We look for their strengths and decide what we can do to counter them. We try to counter a particular team's strengths by making adjustments from our basic defenses. All week we keep going over their basic formations by means of films and scouting reports and everything else. Then when it comes time for the game, we've got a good idea as to what they'll try to do.

"Say this week we're preparing for the 49ers," Dick says. "I'll watch the films of the last 49er game and particularly check out the middle linebacker's play against the 49ers. I'll look at what he does against their center and maybe get a tip or two from how he played it. I'll try to put myself in his position and see what my best abilities are and how I'd work against the San Francisco line."

Butkus watches other middle linebackers to see what he might be able to use, not to copy them. Every individual is a little different in his style of play. "They say Ray Nitschke of the Packers is a real rough, tough player and they say Tommy Nobis of the Falcons is not as rough but he has more speed. Well, you're a little different, too. So you've got to fit yourself in there against that particular offensive line. You've got to try to get tips from other linebackers, but deep down you know the way you play and you try to adapt yourself as to what you're gonna do against this opponent."

For all the preparation, though, the middle linebacker still has to depend on his instinctive knowledge of the game. He's the quarterback of the defense, and he has to know everything that's going on and anticipate anything that might happen. For example, the offensive team is also preparing for *him,* and in a very short time he has to be able to counteract what they are doing. "You might have all the tips in the world, but once you get in a game," Dick says, "they might have a tip on you and try to work on you. If you don't realize this and try to adjust . . . well, it's too late after the game."

Another basic requirement of a middle backer is an intense desire to hit people. "He should feel that he's going to make *every* tackle," Dick says, "no matter where the play starts or ends up. He should make the tackle because he's in the middle of things. But to do so he's got to have a strong desire to make the tackle. He's got to say to himself, 'I'm gonna make this tackle no matter where it's at.' It's not like playing any other position. Take a defensive end. When the opponent sweeps the other way, the defensive end has no chance to make the tackle —at least very seldom. But a middle linebacker—no matter what kind of run it is—must eliminate the blocker and make the tackle. This is just plain desire to always be where the ball's at."

Dick Butkus has had this desire from the sixth grade of grammar school. That was when he decided he wanted to become a professional football player. "That was the only thing

I had in my mind from that time on," Dick says. "I tried to adapt all my playing of sports toward my ultimate goal of playing pro football. I played basketball to get a little more agility. I wrestled to get a little endurance. I played baseball to get a little more speed and improve my running. I didn't weight-lift very much, but I did do heavy-work jobs all the time—construction jobs, furniture-moving jobs. . . . Mentally, I have always studied the game because ever since high school I have always played middle linebacker and, as I say, you have to know what's going on there."

For all Butkus' size, agility, strength and football knowledge, he finds that two plays are especially tough for him to make—the screen pass and the draw play. Both show pass-action initially, which sends the middle linebacker dropping back into his zone. "Then, all of a sudden, the offensive linemen release their blocks and go to one side to set a screen," Dick says. "The offensive back follows behind them and now you've got two, three, maybe four linemen over there in front of the ball carrier. A linebacker has got to react in a hurry to get over, avoid being blocked in the open field and then make an open-field tackle. It's extremely hard to do.

"The draw play is hard because of the same thing. The ball is snapped, you read pass and drop to cover your zone. Then all of a sudden there's a handoff and it's a run. What makes it tough is that you're three or four yards back in the open—all set up for the offensive linemen. The draw and the screen are definitely two of the hardest plays for the middle linebacker to make."

Still, Butkus has made some very important plays on both draws and screens. Back in his rookie season against Baltimore, Butkus fought through a draw block and hit fullback Tony Lorick high. "I don't know how it happened," Dick says, "but when I tackled him my hands wrapped around the ball and, when he went down, I had the ball and started running the other way. It was kind of a weird feeling.

"You can stop the screen by yourself if you recognize it

quick enough. Otherwise you've got to have help—some pursuit from your linemen and from another linebacker. You've got three linemen coming at you and you've got to come up with a really great play to stop the ball carrier alone. If I see I can't make the tackle, I try to take down the interference. The thing is, at times during a game—because of the emotional stress or because maybe you're just caught napping—you might not recognize the screen until it's too late. You feel bad about missing it. But mistakes are part of the game. This is what makes the game so exciting—because there's so much of the human element in it."

The easiest play for Butkus to make, he feels, is on a sweep. Of course, his success depends on the ability of the outside linebacker to force the play inside—right into the arms of the middle linebacker, who's charging up from the inside underneath the blockers. "You should make the tackle on this play every time," Dick says. "In the Pittsburgh game early this season they tried a lot of sweeps and I handled them easily every time. The Rams tried a few sweeps early in the game and we were able to stop them without any trouble and they quit going outside. This is something you like to do—take something away from the other team's offense, narrow down the number of things they can try against you."

In the heyday of the Green Bay Packers, the Lombardi power sweep was one of the team's biggest plays. With guards Jerry Kramer and Fuzzy Thurston pulling and leading Paul Hornung or Jim Taylor, the Packers ran this play successfully in both long-yardage and short-yardage situations from all over the field. With the retirement of its fine guard tandem, Green Bay's sweep went downhill. Then the Cleveland Browns became the most successful sweeping team in the NFL. Guards Gene Hickerson and John DeMarie chopped down the force man and the pursuit while Leroy Kelly or another back ran for big yardage. The Bears prepared for this, however, when playing Cleveland and handled it fairly well, thanks to their linebackers.

"I remember one particularly big play," says Butkus. "It was a short-yardage situation, third and maybe a yard to go, and the Browns tried a sweep with Ron Johnson carrying. I just started moving laterally as I saw him starting to go wide. Leroy Kelly and the two guards were leading the play, but no one blocked down on me. We had a good force by the outside linebacker and Johnson started to cut up through the tackle and end hole for the first down. I just shot through the hole and dropped him for a three-yard loss.

"Those plays really stick in your mind," Dick says, smiling. "Any time you have a crucial play—a short-yardage play on third down or goal-line play—and the middle linebacker is able to stop it . . . well, it just gives you a great lift, a great feeling."

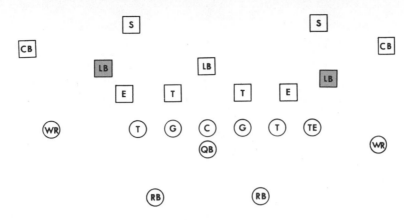

DAVE ROBINSON
Outside Linebacker

A roar spilled down to the field of the crowded Cotton Bowl as the Dallas Cowboys' last-ditch drive rolled closer and closer toward the touchdown that would tie the 1966 title game with the Green Bay Packers. There was less than a minute to play and it was fourth down, but the Cowboys were on the Green Bay two-yard line. Packer linebacker Dave Robinson checked the formation as Dallas broke the huddle. He lined up on speedy flanker Bob Hayes, who set close to the tackle in the tight end's position.

Robinson, a 6-foot-3, 240-pound linebacker, knew that the 185-pound Hayes wasn't there to try to block him. He was going to attempt to get out quickly for a pass or take a Packer defensive back out of the area. So on the snap, Robinson jammed up Hayes at the line, trying to help the Packer secondary. This almost led to disaster, because Dallas quarterback Don Meredith rolled to his right. On a roll-out to the right, Robinson is supposed to race to the sideline to keep the quarterback from turning the corner. Then he drives at him from the outside.

"But by the time I released Hayes," says Dave, "I saw that the pulling guard had overrun me." Robinson blew past the inside of guard Roger Donohue and dragged Meredith down by his left arm as Don threw the pass. It fluttered into the end

zone—right into the arms of a Packer safetyman. With that play, Green Bay earned the honor of representing the NFL in the first Super Bowl.

For his outstanding feat, Dave Robinson received a minus when the films were graded. Vince Lombardi, who was still coaching the Packers at the time, pointed out to Dave that if he had come at Meredith from the outside, as prescribed, he would have grabbed the quarterback's *right* arm.

Robinson, of course, is well aware of the reasoning behind the minus grade. "Coming in behind the guard," he says, "is a very dangerous thing to do. If the guard had gotten back to cut me down there was nobody there to contain the quarterback. So Meredith could have run forever. But sometimes you just feel that, even though it's not the way your defense is drawn up on the board, it's the way to do it. Sometimes you have to change as the play develops. But I can see why they gave me the minus. If you get in the habit of doing these things, it's gonna hurt you more than it will help you. If it's not a habit with you, when you see the opportunity to do it, you'll do it. But if it is a habit, you'll be doing it when you really shouldn't."

You have to know the rules before you can break them, is what Dave Robinson seemed to be saying about playing his position of outside linebacker in the pros. He was relaxing in his Green Bay apartment on the Monday after a shutout victory over the explosive Chicago Bears and superstar Gale Sayers. Robinson's broad face and big eyes were smiling. He exuded the confidence of the true All-League player.

"Now if that had been some other team," Dave continued, making a final point about his play on Hayes, "I wouldn't have overplayed the end so much. A team like Baltimore, say, would have John Mackey on the strong side and Tom Mitchell, a good blocking end, in tight. I'd only hold him up for a split second until I saw the guard pull. Then I'd meet the guard from the outside and force the play in."

The roll-out, in which the quarterback has the option of running or passing, and the run-action pass, in which the quarterback fakes a handoff to a running back and then pulls the ball back and passes, are the toughest plays for Robinson. In both instances he can get caught right in the middle, which just might create a six-point play for the opposition. Suppose he reads run, comes up to stop it and the opponent's quarterback hits one of his running backs in the zone the linebacker is responsible for. Or what if he reads pass, drops back and a ball carrier runs right through the area he's just vacated?

The linebackers are the men quarterbacks attack and attempt to control. They are the key to a defense. As Dave Robinson, an engineer in the off-season, says: "They are the catalysts. Just as you can put hydrogen and oxygen together all day and never get water unless you introduce something like a platinum rod. In the same way, you can have a great defensive line and backfield but, if you've got no linebackers, you have no defense."

Outside linebacker is probably the most complicated position on the defense. This is one reason why Dave Robinson wasn't satisfied with his game until his fourth year as a Packer. An All-America end out of Penn State in 1963, he played very little during his rookie year. The following season he became a starter but injured a knee and had to have an operation. Although he played all of 1965, he was concerned about the knee, at least subconsciously, and "didn't really cut loose." He was also concerned about learning his position.

"It was not a good year," he says. "I'd read pass on almost every play. I ran back anytime the quarterback showed me pass-action." He laughs in retrospect. "There were always *acres* of grass in front of me. Now I feel things. I'll see one, two, three keys that say run but I'll *feel* pass. Then I'll see the last key and know I was right. It's a pass."

The outside linebacker has to read two different sets of keys because, in fact, he plays two different positions, according to how the offense lines up. Robinson plays the left side, which means he's usually opposite the opponent's tight end because most teams are "right-handed." Since the flanker normally sets out of this side, too, it is called the strong side. The other side, which has only one receiver split out on it, is known as the weak side. But teams do flip-flop their receivers so the linebacker must know both jobs.

"On the strong side your primary responsibility is to stop the tight end," says Robinson. "If he's trying to block, you defeat him. If he's trying to release for a pass, you try to hold him up." For openers Dave clubs the tight end on every play. "I like to come up underneath his shoulder pads and club him with my forearm to get him straightened up, then I use my other hand to shed up if I want to. A lot of linebackers, like Bobby Bell of Kansas City and Wayne Walker of Detroit, stand up with both hands out and smack the tight end in the shoulders with a fore-hand shiver. Or they grab the tight end and throw him one way or the other."

Although Walker and Bell are both outstanding backers, Robinson prefers the "club" to the "shiver" for a couple of rea-sons. First, having played a lot of defensive end in high school and college, he's been using his forearm for a great many years. Second, coming up from a crouch with his forearm gets Rob-inson moving quicker.

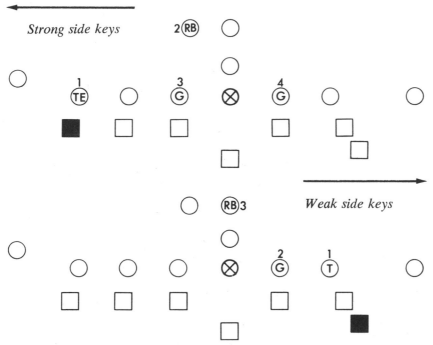

The outside linebacker "reads" the movements of key offensive players to anticipate the offense.

"For me," Dave says, "the difference is that, if you hand-fight him, you kind of stand still nullifying his charge, then you have to move. But when you club the tight end you have a little bit of forward momentum, and this gets me going. Some people do it differently, but for me to be successful I have to keep my feet moving. Once my feet stop, then my whole play goes to pot. I've seen it while watching films. But when I hit with my forearm, one foot comes over and then I bring the other one over and I'm already moving. I just get off quicker."

All the time, of course, he's checking his other keys. The tight end is only the first. Set behind the tight end is the "near" running back, who can block him, go out for a pass on him, or carry the ball. This player is the second key. The third is the near guard. "The fourth is the far guard, if you get that far," says Robinson. "I haven't gotten that far yet. You have no more than seven-tenths of a second to key all these people and start your counterattack, and I never have time to key the far guard. Now Bill Forester, when he played outside linebacker with us, used to key on *six* guys on every play."

As a rookie, Robinson concentrated on the tight end so much that he often had trouble picking up the near-back key. But he couldn't react really effectively until he got the near guard into his reading. For example, there are three running holes inside the end on the strong side—numbered, say, five, seven and nine. When the far back is carrying into any of those holes, the tight end and near back usually double up on the strong-side linebacker. So their actions give Robinson no clue as to which of the three holes the ball's coming through.

"The difference is the guard," says Dave. "On the five play the near guard blocks the tackle and the far guard pulls to get the end. On the seven play the near guard blocks down, but the far guard pulls to block *me*. On the nine play, both guards pull. Sometimes both pull on the seven, with the far hitting the tackle and the near hitting the end. You can tell the hole, though: on the seven play the rear guard doesn't pull as *deep* as he does on the nine."

The outside linebacker's main responsibility after the tight end is the run—everything from the off-tackle play out to the sideline is his. He is also expected to help out on everything from the off-tackle on in. But it's the wide stuff that Dave digs: the tight end cutting at him, the guards coming—with no one over there except the linebacker. He has to turn the play inside or string it out to the sideline. He must keep it from turning upfield until the safetyman or cornerback comes up to "force" the play.

"It's my job to see that by the time the force man gets up, all the blockers have been stripped away. If I don't make the tackle, I've got to strip away the blockers, because even a poor lineman can overpower a little defensive back. If you get even one blocker on a back out there, the play's going to go for a long gainer. I've got to have it stripped so the halfback can attack the runner one-on-one.

"Most teams play it so the force men come up *inside* the linebacker. This means the back's got to release very fast to get up inside, and as a result you can get hurt on a pass play at times. We play it so the force man comes up *outside* me." This means that the Packers' outside backer has to string out the play a little longer, stand in there a little tougher.

After the run, the backer plays the pass. His responsibility is any short pass to the flat or hook zone on his side. And he also must cover the near back—usually the fullback—man to man, long or short, in most defensive calls.

"Here's the difference between a linebacker and a *good* linebacker," says Robinson. "Any linebacker can read pass and run to the flat. That's his job as it's drawn up on the board. But say you're going to the flat and the flanker's out there with nobody outside him. If he starts running a quick slant-in or turn-in, there's no sense in my continuing on out to the sideline. I've got to bump him and come in with him to give my halfback underneath coverage. And it's the same way with the hook—you pick up anybody who comes into your zone."

On the weak side Robinson usually has to cover the speedy

halfbacks "all the way," as they say on television, making it sound near impossible. Most outside linebackers do shudder at the thought, but not Dave. "I'm three yards back on the weak side and the halfback's three yards deep in the backfield, so I've got about a seven-yard head start on him. And he's got to beat me by at least three yards for the quarterback to get the ball over my head. I'm six foot three and I can jump ten feet. Now the farthest a quarterback can throw the ball is about fifty yards from the line of scrimmage. Remember, he's almost ten yards behind it. So we're talking about a fifty-yard dash— and any man who gets beat by ten yards in a fifty-yard dash has to be *walking*. If a halfback can run a nine-flat 100, all I have to run is an eleven-flat and I've got him covered. The speed thing is really not that important."

The only way the linebacker can be beaten is if he starts rushing up just before the ball is snapped and is caught going the wrong way. According to Robinson, the secret is to "stay off the back and let the ball bring you up." That was exactly what Dave had done in his last game against the Bears' Gale Sayers. He stayed off him because he knew Sayers wasn't going to stop just beyond the line for a short pass—not with a linebacker like Robinson waiting to punish him from behind. On the quick pops, Dave just punishes the halfback until he tells the quarterback—or the coach tells him—to stop throwing those passes. A player like Sayers is simply too valuable to risk having him knocked out of the game.

On the weak side, not only the linebacker's coverages but his keys change. "My first key here is the offensive tackle," says Dave. "He's gonna show you run or pass first. [If he blocks across the defensive line, the tackle becomes an 'ineligible receiver downfield' on a pass.] Nowadays, with so many aggressive-type blocks by the lineman on quick turn-ins and hooks, I find I have to key the tackle and the guard. Then I key the near back. Being three yards off the line, you have more time on the weak side. You have time to read, fight off a block and still react up there to stop the run. Also, by looking at the guard, you can tell a draw. The tackle is gonna give you a good pass fake on a draw, and the back is gonna give you a good pass fake. But that guard has to drop back a little bit and then come up and get the middle linebacker.

"The danger comes, of course, when they fake the draw and throw a pass, because the halfback—your man—is gonna run the pass pattern. The fullback runs the draw so he's gonna fake it. If you start overplaying the draw and stop the man a couple of times, then they're gonna fake the draw. The quarterback's gonna pull it out of the fullback's stomach, straighten up and hit your man. But, between you and me, you can read the fake draw pretty easily. That guard isn't gonna go through with his block downfield on the middle linebacker. It's a 15-yard penalty."

There you have the basics of outside linebacker as played by the pros. But one other all-important requirement is a thorough knowledge of the offense. The linebacker has to know every offensive player's assignments so that he can anticipate what they're trying to do to *him*. He must know exactly what the offense can and can't do from every formation. And from his study of films, he must know what a team is most likely to do in any given situation.

"If they come out in what we call a 49 [formation]," says Dave, "from this set they can run a power sweep and an off-tackle. But they can't run the trap in there, they can't run the dive play. I eliminate, narrow it down. Then I watch the tight end's split away from the tackle. If the end's gonna block down on the defensive end, he usually doesn't get more than a yard and a half away. If he's gonna block down on me, he's usually two yards away. Now, if he's split out three yards or more, then he's probably going out for a pass because he can't effectively block from out there. Then there's the weight on the fingers that tells you if they're gonna pass-block or fire out. And if they're up real close to the line, you know they're gonna block: they're trying to get to you quicker. When they do that I back up so I have more time to react.

"On a pass play, they stay back from me, and I'll tell you why—because I club them. I try to club a man on the first play of the game if he's going away from me. I club him as hard as I can if he's going to the other side. Then, when he's not assigned to block you, well, he's human, and in his mind he's saying, 'If he's gonna beat me to death when I'm not assigned to block, I might as well just fake and release every time.' Now to fake, he has to back off a little, so you've set up your key."

Set it up by doing the thing Dave Robinson loves most: hitting people. "That's why I like playing the strong side best," Dave says through a big grin. "The tight end is right there and you know that as soon as the ball is snapped, there's somebody there for you to hit. On the weak side you're three yards off the line and if the play goes away from you, you don't get to hit anybody. I feel more like I'm playing football when I'm hitting people."

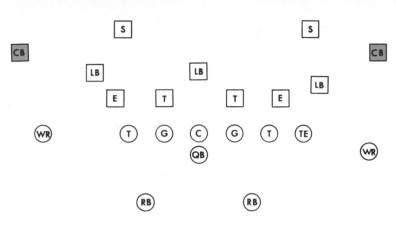

LEM BARNEY
Cornerback

"It's the loneliest spot in the world," says Detroit star Lem Barney. In making such a statement, he is merely echoing the sentiments of every man who has ever played cornerback in professional football. There is a difference, though, with Lem Barney. He doesn't say it sadly, shaking his head. He says it *laughing*.

The only thing you really have to know about the cornerback is that he is responsible for covering the fastest and trickiest men in football. He is faced with players like Bob Hayes, who has run the 100-yard dash in 9.1 seconds, or Lance Rentzel, who has been known to fake defenders right off their feet. Hayes and Rentzel play for the same team—the Dallas Cowboys—and they run from first one side of the field and then the other. As a result, an opposing cornerback can't adjust to the speed of one receiver before he has to readjust to the other's deceptiveness. (In addition, Rentzel is also very fast.) All the cornerback is expected to do is to keep the receiver—who knows precisely where he's going and when the football should be thrown to him—from catching passes.

This kind of pressure has been known to boggle the minds of some men who have tried to play the corner. The Lions had one player who was an outstanding athlete with fine speed and agility. But he'd been strictly an offensive player as a college

All-America. When the Lions tried him at cornerback, the player worked and worked, but he got tighter and tighter. Finally he simply could not run; his legs wouldn't move. Pressure.

But the pressure doesn't bother Lem Barney. When you ask him what kind of receiver he'd prefer to cover—a speedster or a trickster—he looks at you with those serious dark eyes and says, "Well, neither one of them gives me much trouble."

This may sound immodest, but in fact it is just an example of Lem Barney's confidence. Barney feels that confidence is all-important in a cornerback. What else does one need to play the position well?

"Speed helps, but you don't need a whole lot of speed," Lem says. "Quickness is another thing. And agility. Also, being able to back-pedal. Everyone can run forward. It's harder to get down the method of going backward fast. You have to practice that. I devote a lot of time to it. And another thing you've got to have is a little extra sense—for the quarterback."

Barney has been clocked in the 100 in 9.5 seconds, which is fast, though not as fast as the speed of many receivers. That's where quickness and agility and that "little extra sense" for reading the quarterback come in. These things have to make up the difference in speed between the cornerback and the receiver. They also have to make up for all the other advantages the pass-catcher has.

The cornerback is set several yards off the receiver, which is a help. But when the receiver starts on his pattern, faking one way and then the other with full speed, the only thing a defensive halfback can do is back-pedal as fast as possible in order to stay with the receiver. Moreover, the cornerback can't commit himself to going to either one side or the other until he is absolutely sure where the receiver is going. If the cornerback breaks to his right after an end, for example, and the end then cuts back, there is a very good chance the defender will not be in position to knock down the pass. Unless, of course, he is a Lem Barney. Lem is so quick and so instinctive a ballplayer

that he can recover from a wrong move and still get back into position to fight for the ball. Or he will do something to foul up the play.

Consider the move Barney made in an exhibition game against the New York Jets in 1968. Don Maynard, the Jets' speedy flanker, went down the right sideline, faking Lem to the outside, to the inside, and to the outside again. Barney stayed with Don on the first move, but then hesitated on the second and looked as if he would never recover to get back in front of Maynard on the outside. However, Barney not only recovered; he lunged to intercept the ball. He wasn't content merely to break up the play.

Jet quarterback Joe Namath had a lot of stuff on the pass, though. It zonked into Maynard's chest, and Don turned and headed down the sideline.

But Barney wasn't finished. He spun around after his lunge, dashed after Maynard and smacked him from behind. His hand went for the ball peeking out of the crook of Don's arm. It popped loose, Barney grabbed it, spun again and ran some 20 yards in the other direction.

Barney hadn't been fooled at all by Maynard's moves. Having carefully studied films of the Jets' games, Lem knew that Maynard liked to run that particular zig-out pattern. So the young Lion had actually played possum on the second fake. He figured that Namath would be encouraged to throw the ball and then he, Lem Barney, would lunge over and intercept it.

Studying films is still another thing a cornerback must do if he's to keep his job. In that way he learns exactly what the opposition can and cannot do well. "You've got to know your man," says Lem. "You've got to study him every chance you get. If your man's got a favorite outside pattern, then you have to play him strong on the outside. By playing him strong on the outside, you give him a few of the inside patterns. But because he doesn't like them as well you're taking away his strength.

"One of the guys I play strong to the outside is Clifton McNeil. The first year he was with the 49ers his favorite pattern was a drag pattern to the sideline. He might fake going inside or fake going deep, but I'd stay on the outside, just play him tough out there. Willie Richardson of the Colts is one of the tougher men on the inside patterns, particularly the post pattern. He loves to run that. So I play him tough on the inside, hanging in there and forcing him to go outside."

If the receiver doesn't get open, of course, the quarterback won't throw him the ball. And if the receiver keeps running patterns to the side which the cornerback is overplaying, then he may never get open. Eventually the end will have to make a change in his routes. Meanwhile, the receiver is trying to force the cornerback to cover him a certain way. It's all a game of push and tug and guessing.

"The most important part of playing cornerback is not physical but mental," Barney says. "I believe playing the position is 90 per cent mental and only 10 per cent physical. There is always going to be the physical contact; that's to be expected. But the mental part of the game means a lot more. As I said, you've got to know your opponents. You've got to be prepared. What does this team, this quarterback, this receiver like to do in such and such a situation? You study the films and you play the game and you find out."

If you judge football players by their statistics—which can be silly—you might assume that Barney had his greatest season before he had learned much about his opponents. As a rookie in 1967 he intercepted a league-leading ten passes, which he returned for 232 yards and three touchdowns. The latter mark tied an all-time National Football League record for one season. Actually Barney didn't know much about his opponents that first season, and they didn't know much about him. That is why they kept throwing his way. Quarterbacks tend to pick on rookies simply because rookie cornerbacks are usually the softest touches in the game. But Lem kept knocking down passes, intercepting passes and scoring touchdowns on passes. Opponents don't throw much at Detroit's left cornerback anymore.

Barney was the Lions' number two draft choice in 1967—a six-foot, one-inch, 190-pounder out of Jackson State. "I went there as a quarterback," says Lem, "but I got very little playing time my first season. And I wanted to play football so I asked if I could play defensive back. I figured I could play the position. No, it wasn't easy to change positions. But I did it and it wasn't *that* tough."

During his three college seasons Barney intercepted 26 passes. When he wasn't intercepting passes he was studying films of the Green Bay Packer defense which his college coach obtained for him. Lem also watched Packer cornerbacks Herb Adderley and Bob Jeter on television and decided they were the best in football. Why not study the best?

The films helped him when he reported to the Lions, where coach Joe Schmidt didn't think much of Barney's chances to become a starter right away. "It's the most difficult spot on defense," said Joe, "and it takes more time to learn than any other position. Barney's chances of playing this year are pretty slim. Not many come in and play cornerback in their first year."

Barney wasn't concerned. He brought with him the confidence which he feels is so important in playing cornerback. During his very first scrimmage, Lem was covering veteran Lion receiver Gail Cogdill and knocking down one pass after the other. Then Cogdill ran a pattern. Barney stayed right with him and, as the ball descended, Lem reached over the end's shoulder and made the interception one-handed. Someone yelled, "Interference!"

"Offensive or defensive?" said Lem.

When the Lions opened the season in Green Bay, Barney was a starting cornerback. Early in the game quarterback Bart Starr sent his big flanker, Boyd Dowler, out on a pattern against Barney. Dowler raced straight at the young corner-back, driving him backward. But Lem was no more than a yard behind Dowler when he cut sharply toward the sideline. The pass was thrown low and to Dowler's inside. Barney's cleats dug into the field as he stopped short.

"I dove for the ball, tumbled over, came up with it and ran into the end zone for a touchdown," Lem recalls. "I'll never forget that play. It will probably always stand out in my mind as the best play I ever made."

He doesn't recall other big plays he's made, but he remembers the ones he's been beaten on. "I can recall *them* all right," he says. "Most of them came when I was taking a chance and I can recall just what I did wrong. The one that comes to mind first was against Clifton McNeil in my second season. As I said before, he runs good outside patterns, but this time he went inside on a deep post. I was in front of him but I gambled a bit and went for the interception. I cut in front of him, but it was a good pass and I couldn't reach it. He caught it and I tried to tackle him as I went down. I missed and he went in to score. The thing is, if you're going to gamble, you know you're going to get burned once in a while. You can't let it bother you. You've just got to know when to gamble and when not to."

Although the cornerback is primarily responsible for guarding against passes, he also has responsibilities on running plays. He works with the safetyman on his side. One rushes in and forces the play while the other holds his ground and contains.

"It depends on the split the receiver takes as to who forces the play and who contains," says Lem. "If the receiver isn't

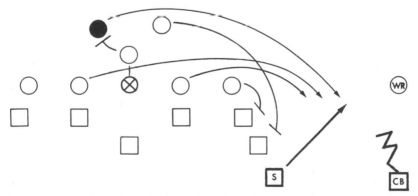

On a sweep, when the wide receiver is split more than ten yards, the safety (S) forces the play from the inside, while the cornerback (CB) contains, keeping play from turning outside.

split out wide—up to ten yards from the tackle—then it's the corner's job to force. If the receiver splits out more than ten yards, the corner's out too far to force. Then the safety will force and I will contain.

"Different teams have different methods of force and contain. Some other teams use their linebackers for containment. But basically, my job with the Lions is to contain on the run."

This can be a painful business for a smaller man—rushing in and stripping away blockers who are at least 50 pounds heavier. There are even times when the pursuit doesn't get over quick enough—say, on a sweep. In that case the cornerback has to get past the blockers and take the runner by himself. Whirling around blockers and then diving at a ball carrier can leave the cornerback in an awkward position to make a tackle. In 1968 Barney had to make such a tackle on Gale Sayers of the Bears.

"I didn't have any support. I was all by myself," Lem recalls. "When I got to Gale my body was extended fully and I hit him around his knees. I made the tackle, but I couldn't get up for a little while. . . ."

The first time Barney played against the Bears in 1967, he gained the distinction of being one of the few men ever to catch Sayers from behind. The tackle saved a touchdown. During the next Chicago series, Sayers popped through the line into daylight, but was quickly shadowed by Barney. Lem drove in low and dropped Gale after a two-yard gain. When they got up, Lem grabbed Sayers' right hand and gave it a strange-looking shake.

"That was our fraternity grip," Barney confided after the game. "Gale was Kappa Alpha Psi at Kansas and I was the same at Jackson State. But don't tell the coach. . . . He might not want me consorting with opponents."

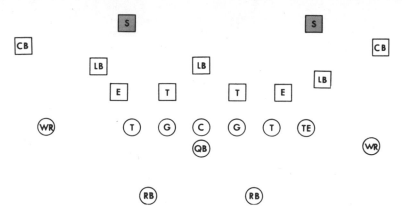

RICK VOLK
Safety

"The first responsibility of all your defensive backs—both safeties and cornerbacks—is to stop the pass and, secondarily, to stop the run," says Rick Volk. Rick plays the right, or what is called the "weak" or "free," safety position for the Baltimore Colts. Since most teams are right-handed, the tight end sets mostly on the right side—and that becomes the strong side. So the left safety is called the strong side or tight safety. He covers the tight end, man-to-man. The right safety is then playing on the weak side. He is known as the free safety because he doesn't have to cover anyone man-to-man unless a running back comes out of the backfield on a deep pass pattern.

"If you don't have man-to-man responsibilities you can just roam the field and play the eyes of the quarterback," says Rick. "Where the strong safety has definite responsibilities, you're more free on the weak side. But it's gotten so the weak-side safety is hardly ever free anymore. I know here at Baltimore, we have weak-side responsibilities most of the time even when we're not covering a back man-to-man. We have to help out the cornerback, for example. Now, while you're doing this, you're also trying to read the pattern and trying to read the quarterback's eyes. That will usually tell you where the problem's going to be. As soon as you read where the play's going to go, you can free up and get over there. You try to help out

wherever it's needed.

"The quarterback is reading, too, trying to see where there's a breakdown in the defense, where a receiver seems to be getting open. When they see a breakdown, they'll throw that way. If you can read the quarterback's eyes, then you should be where the breakdown is."

Because almost every team has a pair of exceptional wide receivers, the weakside safety has had to help the right cornerback more and more. In the early 1960s the free safety was a kind of centerfielder who read the quarterback's eyes on virtually every play and simply played the ball. This is one reason why free safeties like Larry Wilson, Jimmy Patton and Paul Krause were consistently among the interception leaders at season's end.

"Now we help out the cornerback on the inside before we can free up," says Volk. "Often we double-team the wide receiver. We have inside and outside responsibility. I take the inside move of the receiver and the cornerback will take the outside move. But once the receiver has committed himself to an outside move, then I'm free to help out elsewhere because I know the cornerback's been playing him to the outside."

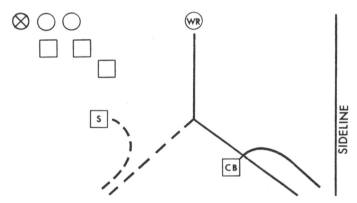

Double-team pass coverage: the cornerback covers outside patterns (solid lines) and the safety covers inside patterns (dotted lines).

Against the Detroit Lions in his rookie year, 1967, Volk had inside responsibility on split end Pat Studstill. Rick backpedaled as Studstill came straight down the field. Then Pat cut to the outside. Seeing that Colt cornerback Lenny Lyles was in good position to cover Studstill, Volk looked in at the quarterback and then cut across the field to help out his left cornerback. The Lion flanker was running a Z-in pattern deep down the middle. Volk read it, cut in front of the flanker as the ball arrived and intercepted it. Obviously the Lion quarterback had seen Volk on the other side when he decided to pass, never figuring the safety would read the pattern quickly enough to get over in front of the pass.

"The new offenses now are trying to isolate a safety on a real fast receiver," says Rick. He runs the 100-yard dash in 10-flat and therefore couldn't possibly play cornerback, where he'd have to cover much faster receivers from the line of scrimmage all the way to the goal line.

"In our last game with Dallas, Lance Rentzel and Bob Hayes were on the same side," says Rick. "*My* side. Usually they run a combination pattern. One will do an outside move and one will do an inside move. Or one will go straight down the field and the other guy will cut underneath [in front of] him, where the other guy has cleared out. It's hard to cover these guys man-to-man. But if you know you've got help to the outside, you can cheat to the inside and concentrate on where your coverage should be. Hayes is so much faster than I am it's silly. But if I have deep inside responsibility, I'll just take the inside and drop back. He'll be running to me instead of away from me.

"On this particular play [in the game with Dallas], Hayes came down and ran an inside move on me while the other receiver went outside. The ball was thrown to Hayes and it was a little behind him. I was able to step in and intercept it because I knew what to expect and I was in position. But they're definitely changing to this type of offense to try to take advantage of the safety, who is not used to covering people with a lot of moves and a lot of speed."

Volk feels that speed is a necessity in a safety, but not the burning speed that is a necessity for a cornerback. "I think you've got to be really quick both physically and mentally," he says. "You have to be able to read plays and read your keys and know what you have to do. Knowing your responsibilities, knowing your defense and having the desire is more important than speed, I think. You can't be really slow and play safety. But you could be the fastest guy around and if you don't know the defense, your team will be hurting. I think a 4.7 or 4.8 in the 40-yard dash is a good time for a safetyman, and if you can run it faster that's great. But you've got to have something on the ball. You've got to have desire and you have to want to hit. Then the rest of it will kind of fall into place. If you have the desire to go out and hit, and you exert the effort, you're gonna be good. I think I've always had the desire."

Rick Volk's desire may come from his solid football background. His uncle, Bob Chappius, was an All-America at Michigan; and his brother-in-law, Bill Laskey, plays linebacker with the Oakland Raiders. A quarterback in high school, Rick became a defensive halfback and safetyman at the University of Michigan, where he played well enough to be drafted on the second round by the Colts. The regular Colt free safety, Alvin Haymond, dislocated his shoulder before the 1967 exhibition season started. So almost as soon as Volk reported from the College All-Star camp, he was a regular for the Baltimore team. "I came in in the second half of the first exhibition game and I've been there ever since," says Rick.

During Volk's rookie year, coach Don Shula said, "It takes an unusual type of player to comprehend everything, to absorb what we try to teach and retain his poise at the same time. There's a lot for a rookie to be thinking about out there— reading the opponent's offense, knowing what he's supposed to do and being able to react. But Rick is a 'big play' guy."

Rick demonstrated this early in his rookie season. The Colts were leading the Bears, 10-3, but Chicago had driven down to the Baltimore six-yard line. The Bears' running back, Brian Piccolo, swung out of the backfield on a pass route and Volk, playing in tight, picked him up, man-to-man. Johnny Morris, the Bear flanker, came cutting by Volk on a crossing pattern, trying to screen Rick. But the Colt safety stayed with Piccolo, looked back over his shoulder as the ball was released and lunged in front of Piccolo to make the interception. He ran it back 94 yards for a touchdown to lock up the game for Baltimore.

That play started with a fake handoff to a running back. This puts a lot of pressure on the safetymen because they have to worry about the run as well as the pass. If a ball carrier gets past the linebackers, there is no one else in the middle to stop him except the safeties.

"The play-action pass is more difficult than the straight drop-back pass because you've got to be concerned about the run," says Rick. "But if you're playing your right defense and reading your keys properly, you're not gonna get messed up by that play action. Playing weak safety, I usually just key the quarterback. If I see it's going to be a pass I look to the receivers and try to figure out the pattern they're going to run.

"This happens real quick. As soon as the quarterback gets the ball, you can usually tell whether he's handing it off or dropping back to pass. It's probably a full second before you can tell what's really going to happen. You're not just standing still, though; you're moving as you're reading. Where you're moving depends on the situation. Say, if it's third-and-ten, they're probably going to be passing, so you're dropping back to cover your first responsibility: stopping the pass. All the time you're reading and, if it is a pass, you keep on dropping to help on a receiver. If it's not a pass, you stop and come up to try and help on the run."

When the tight end sets on the left side of his line, then Volk becomes the tight safety. Some teams flip-flop their safetymen, having the same man play "free" all the time and the other man play the tight end all the time. The Colt safetymen play their side of the field and take what comes.

"When I'm playing strong safety," says Rick, "I try to look at the tight end and then look on back to see what the quarterback and the offensive backs are doing. Keying these guys will usually tell you what's going to happen. The toughest play for a strong safety, I think, is a sweep where you have to come up and force the play. You might have to take on the guard or tackle all by yourself. Or the linemen may block somebody else and then you've got to take the back by yourself.

"The toughest thing to read at strong safety is the tight end's block. Is he really blocking down for a run or is he blocking for one or two counts and then releasing for a pass? If it's a pass you've got to cover him. If it's a run you've got to get in your lane and cover your area to make the tackle. In our last game against the Cowboys, for example, if I hadn't been in my lane the runner would have gone for a big gain. I was the strong safety, and the tight end blocked down on a sweep to my side. I was coming up underneath and we had a good contain on the play. The linebacker was out there and the corner-back came up very fast. The runner saw this and tried to cut back inside, but I was in my lane and made the tackle. Against the Rams the following week we did the same thing. They ran a sweep. We had a good contain, the back came inside and I was able to make the tackle.

"But then when we played the 49ers, they were giving us a little different look. We call it a 39-sweep crackback. The flanker comes back and hits either the linebacker or the safety. They line up the flanker so he is in a little closer. When you try to come up and run in your lane, the guy comes across and tries to knock you right out of the play. Then the back can cut right up in there where you should be and go for extra yard-age. I've had a number of those, too, where they've gotten me.

"Usually you remember your worst plays. Then you can try to make corrections. If you're aware of that flanker soon enough, he shouldn't get you."

Rick Volk feels his strongest asset is probably his ability to read offenses. He's been doing it since college, and he studies films and scouting reports all the time. This, coupled with practice and game experience, helps him keep up with the different looks the offense is always trying to show. "But I still break down," he admits. "You see the films the next day and you know you can do it. You only wonder, 'Why didn't I see that?' These are the things that make you have gray hairs."

The thing he enjoys most about free safety is blitzing. "It's a lot of fun," he says, "and we've had a lot of success with it. We do it maybe three or four times a game. On all blitzes you have

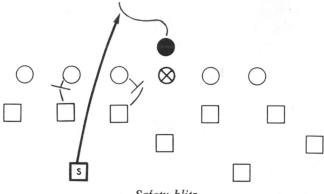

Safety blitz.

a definite place to go. The other guys are trying to make a hole for you to go through. Most of the time on a blitz you don't have any responsibility other than getting to the quarterback, which is the way I like it best. On some blitzes, though, you have pass responsibility if the tight end releases. That's a controlled blitz. If he blocks, you blitz. But on the all-out blitzes, you forget about covering anyone and just go as hard as you can to get the quarterback. That's what I like to do."

The hardest tackle the six-foot-three, 195-pound Volk ever made came on a quarterback. But he didn't make that tackle on a blitz. It happened during an exhibition game against the Oakland Raiders when Daryle Lamonica dropped back to pass. He couldn't find a receiver open so he ran up the middle. Volk raced in and hit Lamonica so hard he had to be helped off the field. "I'm not mean," says Rick, "but I did want to remind him that he really shouldn't be running. He didn't even try to get to the sidelines like most quarterbacks do when they run."

A couple of tight ends named Smith have given Volk the

most trouble when he's been at strong safety. "Jackie Smith of the Cardinals and Jerry Smith of the Redskins—when he moves inside—are both very fast, very fine receivers. I remember one play against Jerry Smith where I was very lucky. The previous week he had caught three touchdowns against the Rams, all on bull-outs to the corner. I think the Redskins had tied L.A. Anyway, I was very conscious of his outside move. In this game against us, he gave me a little outside move and then broke it inside and was wide open. He probably would have scored, but he dropped the pass. This is something he never does, so I was just lucky.

"But we think we've got the best tight end in the business in John Mackey. We go up against him every day in Baltimore, so that's good training for us. He's helped me a lot, because you've got to concentrate a lot more on patterns and things when you're going against a receiver who's All-Pro every year. If you can cover John Mackey, you should be able to cover other people."

Offensive

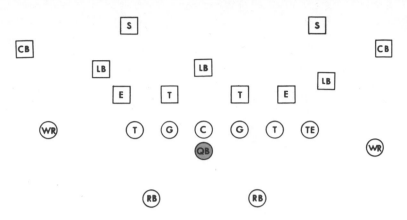

SONNY JURGENSEN
Quarterback

"I consider pro football one of the most difficult professions in the world," says Christian Adolph Jurgensen III, better known as Sonny. "It requires more time and dedication than practically any job I know, because the demands are both physical and mental, particularly for the quarterback."

Sonny Jurgensen has been a quarterback longer than he cares to remember. He put in four years at Duke University, with the great passing arm he still has. But he got little chance to use it because of the running offense that was emphasized there. As an Eagle rookie in 1957 he played well, leading Philadelphia to victories in four of its last five games. But the team acquired Norm Van Brocklin in 1958 and Sonny sat on the bench, observing the old master for the next three seasons. He was more than ready to take over when Van Brocklin retired, and even came within a half-game of taking the Eagles to a championship in 1961.

Although Sonny set all kinds of NFL passing records, the Eagles fell on bad times. In 1963 he was traded to the Washington Redskins, where he continued to set passing records despite weak teams.

"First and foremost," says Sonny, "the quarterback has to be able to throw the ball, which is a God-given talent. He also has to have quickness of arm and feet, along with intelligence.

By that, I mean he has to have football sense that allows him to read defenses and to make adjustments. And he has to have leadership ability.

"Quickness of arm and quickness of feet are very important in throwing the ball, because you have to be able to throw when off balance. You can't always just drop back, set up, step in the direction you're throwing to and then release the ball. You're not always set up to throw the ball when you have to get rid of it. Sometimes, when you're stepping one way, you have to be able to deliver the ball another way. Quarterbacks who work with slow, deliberate motions have to step in the direction they throw, and as a result they get in trouble under any rush. That's why quickness of arm is so important. The quick, supple arm can get the ball off under any pressure, because the player doesn't have to be well set."

In his first season as an Eagle regular, Sonny let everyone know about his supple arm and ability to react under pressure. Against the College All-Stars, Jurgy took the snap. As he dropped back to pass, a defender was in on his right side before Sonny could cock his arm. So he passed the ball behind his back to his halfback on the left side.

Later that season he was pressured by the Redskins, one of whom grabbed his right arm as he was about to pass. Sonny snatched the ball out of his right hand with his left hand, half turned, and threw the ball, left-handed, to halfback Billy Barnes 12 yards away. Barnes made a 27-yard gain. Few quarterbacks have ever shown this kind of dexterity and quick thinking. Against a big rush, Jurgensen has consistently been able to hold the ball to the very last second, until defenders are right on top of him. Only then does he flick the ball away. Still, he feels that at least one other quarterback has an even quicker arm than his.

"Joe Namath of the Jets is the great example of the quick arm," says Jurgensen. "He can throw quickly, he can throw off balance, he can throw while still moving back. And Joe has very quick feet, which is also important. He drops back there so fast that he can get the ball away before even the best rush can reach him. Other people like myself drift back and throw through the gaps in the rush line. The linemen are all so tall now that, when they take a few steps toward you and throw up their arms, you can't pass over them. So you have to pass between them. I don't set up as quickly as Joe or some of the other quick ones. I learned my drop-back from Norm Van Brocklin when I played with him at Philadelphia. In those days the linemen weren't quite as tall.

"But I'm fortunate that I can throw off-balance, from the weirdest positions. I can throw overhand, three-quarter, sidearm. I have to in order to get the ball in between the rush men. That's why I slide around a lot back there, from side to side. The linemen are so tall that I've got to find an alley. This means I'm frequently leaning sideways when I get rid of the ball."

As a result, when throwing, he's probably off-balance more than any other quarterback, but it doesn't affect the velocity of his passes. Sonny, who throws mostly with his wrist, snaps off the football the way pitchers snap off fastballs. He gets the ball to his receivers in a hurry. Receivers, of course, appreciate this. They do not like to make their cut on a pattern and then have to stand there, with their backs to the charging defender, and wait for the football to float out to them. They want to turn and get hit in the belly with the ball before the defensive back or linebacker hits them in the back. Since the pass can be completed either way—by floating or zipping the ball—this may be regarded as a small thing. But the health and happiness of one's receivers are very important to a quarterback's passing game. There are a lot of seemingly small things a quarterback needs to know and usually acquires only through experience.

"For instance," Jurgensen says, "a standard pattern is for a receiver to go straight down and then cut across the field. There are three linebackers he is cutting behind, which means there are two gaps to throw into. There is a gap between the first and second linebackers, and another between the second and third linebackers. A young quarterback who is anxious to get rid of the ball when he sees an open receiver is likely to throw through the first gap. I'm more likely to wait now until he reaches the second gap, because I've learned that it's usually bigger.

"Another thing: when a corner linebacker goes back on pass coverage, he doesn't go straight back. He sort of naturally angles toward the sideline. So you know he's always going to be covering the outside short and you have to pass somewhere else. It's a small thing, but there's such a narrow margin of error in the throwing game anyway that even the smallest thing is significant.

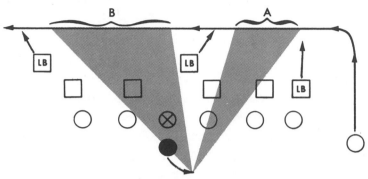

On short pass patterns Jurgensen watches the gaps between linebackers. He prefers to wait and pass through the larger gap (B).

"In every case," Jurgensen says, "the defense tells the quarterback when, where and how to throw the football." The rush, of course, tells him when. The faster the rush, the faster he must get rid of the ball. A couple of years ago, Jurgensen could see from films of the Los Angeles Rams that their great rush line was killing quarterbacks. In the early sixties the passer could figure on 3.5 to 4 seconds as the time he had to get off his pass. So pass patterns were designed to open up in about three seconds. But when the Redskins played against the Rams, the Washington team ran patterns that opened in two seconds or less. Jurgy was rushed unmercifully. The front four knew he was forced by Washington's lack of a running attack to pass up to 50 times per game, and thus they ignored the run and came at him flat out on every play. In spite of the pressure, he was dropped for a loss only once. The Redskins defeated the Rams, and a study of the film later revealed that Jurgensen had gotten off his passes in *1.5 seconds!*

59

The defense tells the quarterback how to throw the ball by the way it reacts. If, for example, the defender plays deep, staying behind the receiver, the quarterback must fire the pass. If the defender plays in front, the quarterback must loop the ball over his head.

The defense also tells the quarterback where to throw the ball by the way in which the defensive players are aligned. "You know what defenses each team uses from studying their game films," says Jurgensen. "Your game plan tells you pretty much what plays you're going to call and when you're going to call them, depending on what the defense shows you in given situations. And on the actual calling of plays, a quarterback gets a lot of help from the staff on the sidelines and particularly from the coaches up in the press box. They've got the best view of what the defense is doing and they suggest what should go.

"Of course, no matter how good your game plan or your information is, you still have to make many adjustments on the field. Which is why I say having football sense and being able to read defenses are so important. You have to be able to read zone, or weakside kick zone or man-to-man coverage, or combo coverage and all the rest. First, you look at the defensive line and see whether they're in an odd defense or an even defense. You know what you're going to do versus an odd defense and what you're going to do versus an even defense.

"Then you look farther and check the linebacker alignment and right on back into the secondary to see what they're doing. Is the linebacker cheating a bit to make a quick pass drop? Is a safetyman shading one way or the other? The defense tries to hide what it's going to do until the last moment, so you've got to pick it up quickly. And you don't actually look at each man. You don't have time. It's a second-nature thing when you come up to the ball. It's almost something you sense or feel. That's why experience and studying the game films are so important.

"The play-calling all depends on what the defensive team is

giving you. I think John Unitas said it best when he said, 'You have to take what the defense gives you.' In order for the defense to take something away from you, it has to give you something. The idea is to know what they're trying to do. The defense is always guessing what you're going to do, and you're always guessing what they're doing. It's a guessing game all along the line."

Like every other quick-release quarterback who's been playing for a number of years, Jurgensen loves to go against a blitzing team. "Teams are getting away from that now, I'm sorry to say," Sonny comments. "Teams are covering up weaknesses if they blitz a lot. Either their rush lines aren't effective or they're weak in the secondary. A quarterback looks forward to playing against a blitz because he throws against one-on-one coverage. You can protect yourself from getting dumped by keeping your backs in to block. Heck, you can keep everybody in except one man. The defense is the one that's gambling.

"The teams with the tough defenses to throw against are the ones with the seven men back there covering and the front four rushing real well. Those are the sound defensive teams. Look at Dallas, for example. How much do the Cowboys blitz? How much does Green Bay blitz? Or L.A., or Minnesota?"

Though the blitz is in decline, the rush lines are better than ever and Jurgensen, a 6-foot 205-pounder, feels size is a great asset in a quarterback. "Size is a key to durability. If you have height, it's easier to see the receivers; and the strength and weight often can keep you from being hurt. Quarterbacks like Roman Gabriel of the Rams, Craig Morton of the Cowboys and Joe Kapp of the Vikings have a great advantage with their height, weight and strength. They all stand about six-four and weigh about 225. They can see over those rushing linemen and see how the secondary is playing. Because of their size and strength, they can take the punishment that all quarterbacks have to take. This is a great attribute for them."

Jurgensen, who has had four operations, believes a quarterback must be philosophical about injuries. "You know you are a target," he says. "Anytime they can get the quarterback out of there, it messes up a team's timing, rhythm. And a quarterback is vulnerable because he is often standing back there exposed, defenseless. He's throwing the ball, his arm is up and there is no way for him to brace himself or protect himself from the impact that's always coming. So quarterbacks get hurt.

"I remember throwing a ball in the play-off bowl in January, 1962, against the Lions. The pass hung a little and was intercepted by Yale Lary, who started down the sidelines. I ran over, trying to force him out of bounds. But their linebacker on that side, Wayne Walker, was running with Lary, trying to block for him. Walker hollered for Yale to cut back so he could block me. I heard him and I tried to turn, but I didn't turn enough. If I had, Walker would have just run over me. But he hit me from the side and completely separated my shoulder—kind of messed me up for a year or two. I had to have an operation to tie my arm back together.

"In Cleveland I got hit one time on a screen pass and it messed me up, too. This was a more typical injury for a quarterback. Paul Wiggin [a defensive end] hit me real hard, but it wasn't the blow so much as the fact that he hit my arm while I was throwing. That's more bothersome than anything else. You don't mind your body getting beaten up so much, but you make your living with your arm. I think I suffered some elbow damage that time. It weakened my arm for several years."

All football players learn to play with injuries, but this is particularly true of quarterbacks. In 1968 Jurgensen's ribs were so severely damaged early in the season that he had to play the rest of the schedule wearing a cumbersome corset-like protective pad. Every time he got hit his ribs ached. This is part of a quarterback's job, the kind of leadership he must show. All the more so when he plays for Vince Lombardi, whose quarterbacks have always been an extension of him on the field.

"You have to be a leader by example," Sonny says, "and this comes only through experience. I can remember being questioned in the huddle when I was a rookie calling plays. A lineman said, 'Hey, rookie, do you think this play is going to work?' And I said, 'Yes, I think it's going to work or I wouldn't have called the play. And it better work.' But football has changed a lot since I was a rookie. It's become a science. You have highly intelligent players now, and it requires more to be a leader than just screaming and hollering at every individual on the field. As a quarterback, I have to consider everyone's personality, know the ones I can *ask* something from and the ones I have to holler at to get what I need. There are even some you have to beg. It comes down to their belief in you as a quarterback, something that doesn't come very easily."

It comes easiest to the great quarterbacks. And what separates the great quarterbacks from the rest? "The personnel he's playing with," Jurgy says, laughing.

"No," he goes on seriously, "the big play for the quarterback—the one that separates the great ones from the others—is the third-and-long play. That's when you have to throw to keep possession of the ball and the other team knows it. Your teammates know it, too, and they're looking to you for the right call. You have to be able to do this time and time again, and this is the greatest pressure on a leader, the toughest test of a quarterback.

"John Unitas has always done this exceptionally well, taking his team on to win in the closing minutes of ballgames. Bobby Layne did it well, too, utilizing every second and every inch of the field to take his team in to win. Norm Van Brocklin was another who was great at it. You can't make any mistakes in these situations; there is absolutely no room for errors. The real good quarterbacks are outstanding in these critical drives."

Unitas, Sonny feels, is the greatest quarterback he's seen. "He works hard at the game, he works hard at excelling, at making the big plays. Anyone who wants to excel, who wants to be the best, has to put out the effort, and this is something John has done year in and year out. Physically, John sets up quickly. He has the God-given talent to throw the ball and, because of his quickness, he is usually well balanced when he throws. Rather than wait to throw, as some quarterbacks do, John is a timing type of passer who likes to anticipate his receivers' moves. This is a big advantage." (See the chapter on wide receiver Clifton McNeil.)

Jurgensen is a pocket-passer just as Norm Van Brocklin was. ("Like him, I run only out of sheer fright.") But Sonny appreciates the fact that a scrambling quarterback can build some time in the face of a great rush to get off passes that pocket throwers would have to eat. "I think Fran Tarkenton does this exceptionally well because he's still looking to throw the ball when he scrambles. Some others just run with the ball before the pattern has time to develop. This, of course, is a busted play. Every time a quarterback scrambles it is a broken play. It's more difficult for his linemen to block and it's hard on his receivers because they have to come off their patterns and also scramble to get open. I'm sure that scrambling is a last resort, even in Tarkenton's case. He would prefer to stand back there and complete passes rather than run around and take a chance on getting hurt. But he had this scrambling ability when he started, and he started with an expansion team that probably didn't give him a lot of time to pass. He seems to scramble less and less every year."

So Sonny wouldn't recommend scrambling—except in pure desperation—any more than he would recommend busted plays as a way to win football games. However, both can produce—at least in retrospect—humorous moments, of which there are very few on a football field.

"I can remember one busted play that seems amusing now, though I can assure you it wasn't at all funny at the time," Jurgy says. "I called a screen pass to Joe Don Looney against Cleveland. Looney had just come in and hadn't really had an opportunity to warm up. I rolled out one way, and the screen rolled the other way. I kept rolling and looking for him, rolling and looking . . . but there was no Joe Don Looney. I kept looking back over my shoulder as I moved across the field and finally I realized I was getting near the sidelines. Then I looked in that direction—and he was standing right next to me. He was still pouting over the fact that he hadn't gotten into the game sooner and hadn't warmed up. I hit him right in the chest with the ball."

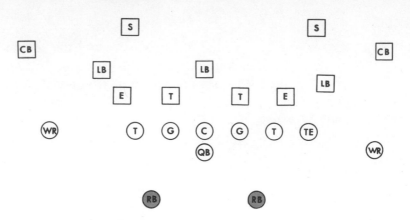

LEROY KELLY
Running Back

For many years the ideal pro football running back was about six feet, one inch tall, weighed about 190 pounds and was very quick on his feet. Until the late 1950s, men like Hugh McElhenny and Frank Gifford were regarded as the perfect ball carriers. Then, as players in other positions—particularly on the defense—became both larger and faster, Coach Vince Lombardi of the Green Bay Packers decided he would use only big running backs. Men like Paul Hornung and Jim Taylor—215- to 225-pounders—set a new style, which other teams soon tried to emulate. "Elephant" backfields popped up all over pro football.

But eventually the trend toward size in running backs began to reverse itself. The change may have begun when Jim Brown unexpectedly retired from football just prior to the 1966 season. Suddenly the Cleveland Browns were forced to replace him with a six-foot, 200-pound runner named Leroy Kelly. During Kelly's first two seasons with the Browns, he had carried the ball from scrimmage fewer than 50 times. His running-back partner, Ernie Green, hadn't done much ball-carrying either while playing alongside Brown. But despite the fact that he weighed only 205 pounds at a height of six feet, one inch, Green had developed into an excellent blocker. He, too, was just waiting for the chance to run with the ball.

By mid-season of 1966 Kelly and Green had set a new style for pro football runners. As the Browns' assistant coach, Dub Jones, said at the time: "They have brought about the realization that you don't need big running backs to have a strong ground attack. Until now people had the feeling that it was crucial to have a lot of size in the backfield. Kelly has shown that you can never sacrifice quickness and coordination for size."

Kelly says, "Size is fine if you're a Jim Brown [6-foot-2, 230 pounds]. But there was only one Jim Brown. It was a wonderful feeling just being on the field with him. You learned by just watching him. The way he would get out quick on a pitchout . . . not waiting for someone to block the defensive end, breezing right past him. The way he snapped his head when he made his move, those first few steps, so quick and yet so controlled. . . ." Kelly shakes his head.

"But you want to know about the basic responsibilities of being a running back. Well, first of all you have to be able to run. You have to have good speed and good moves and you have to be able to run under control and stay with your blockers. The speed and the moves, I think, come naturally to most good runners and aren't taught. I don't think you can learn to make a move on a man or a head fake. But a running back must also be able to catch the football, and he must have enough weight and sufficient desire to block defensive ends and linebackers. A running back can certainly learn how to block, and he can learn how to improve his pass-catching. He can also be taught how to follow his blockers and make the best use of them."

Kelly, watching Jim Brown from the bench for two seasons, learned from a master. That is why he looks much like a small carbon copy of the NFL's all-time rushing leader. Kelly, like Brown, has a fantastically quick start, blasting off so fast that at times he seems to be by the quarterback before he can hand off. In fact, several times during his first season as a regular, Kelly was called for moving before the ball was snapped. The Browns claimed that he wasn't going in motion early, that he simply started faster than anyone else and *seemed* to be in motion. They had to show the officials films to prove their point.

Like Brown, Kelly also runs under very strict control. He zooms up to a hole, then almost stops for a split second to read the defense, see how it's reacting and determine, in turn, how he should react to pick up the most yardage. Kelly runs right on his blocker's backside. He stays there until the moment the block is thrown, then he cuts away.

"It's very important to stay just the right distance from your blocker," Leroy says. "You can be either too far from him or too close. This came up when we looked at the film of the opening game of the 1969 season. I had to sit out the game because of a hamstring pull. Ron Johnson, [the Browns' number one draft choice from Michigan] had a very fine game [100 yards rushing]. But we noticed that he was a little too far away from the pulling guard on sweeps."

As a result, the guards couldn't protect him properly. It's very important for the back to stay close because he makes the guard's job easier by setting up the block. If the runner is right behind the guard and doesn't commit himself, the defender has to hold his ground and try to fight off the blocker or cut him down. In either case the runner should get past this point.

"I personally like to stay real close to the blocker," says Kelly. "Because I'm running under control all the time and I can move to either side of him in a hurry. I can even give the guard a little push and guide him right into the defender, telling the blocker which way to take the man. I'd say a distance of about two yards is right on a sweep or a pitchout—no farther. Then you can break to either side off the block.

"Now, on an inside play like off-tackle or up the middle, there's a definite hole you hit quick so you really don't have much choice about where to run. The hole's either there or it isn't there. Sometimes it'll close so fast that you can bounce out of there and maybe swing outside. But usually when there's no hole you're down on the ground right away.

"When you're going wide and have a blocker out in front of you, you do have a choice about where to go. Before the game you watch the films of your opponent's games and you see how the cornerbacks like to play the sweep. Some like to force inside [come up fast on the inside of the field], hoping the pur-

69

suit gets you. Some play the blockers and try to get you on either side of the guard. They try to get past the guard before he can hit them. And some will come up and just cut the guard away [throw themselves into the guard's legs]. If you're too close to him, then both of you go down. It pays to watch the films closely during the week so that you'll know what to expect from the cornerbacks and how to set them up.

"Say the cornerback has a tendency to force the play inside. You might make him think you're going to the inside, fake in and then go to the outside. Then the next time you might fake outside and go inside."

The running back can do this same kind of setting up of a defender on quick-opening plays up the middle, too. Against the Minnesota Vikings in 1967, for example, the Browns' passing game wasn't going at all, but the running attack led by Kelly pulled Cleveland to within three points of the Vikings. Then, with less than four minutes to play, Cleveland got the ball again on the Minnesota 41. The call was a sweep to the left with Kelly carrying. The guards pulled, Kelly cut in off the first block, then out off the second and went 30 yards down the sideline.

The next play was what Cleveland calls a 22. It started just like a sweep. The quarterback turned and handed to Kelly again, going to his left and the guards again pulled to that side. The middle linebacker, keying on Kelly, slid over to get into the sweep early this time. But on his third step to his left,

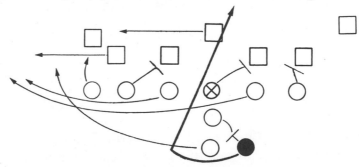

Kelly's fake sweep.

Leroy suddenly planted his left foot and cut back sharply into the middle—right through the area the middle linebacker had vacated. The Viking middle linebacker was now trying to get untangled from the Browns' center, who had come out and nailed him as a result of the angle set up by Kelly. Leroy ran to the three-yard line, and two plays later he dove across the goal line for the game-winning touchdown.

"Except down near the goal line," says Kelly, "when you run through the line you're in relatively open field. Then the idea is not to give the defensive man a big part of your body to hit at. You're planting your foot and taking it away from him, making the defensive man think you're there when you're somewhere else. This is definitely important for the smaller running back like myself. I use moves and speed to try to keep the defensive man from getting close to me. When he does get close, I use a forearm or a straight arm to try to keep him away from my body. The only time I ever try to run over a defender is when he's right on top of me and I have no other choice.

"Now, your big backs have a different style. A lot of them don't have the agility or the moves to go around defenders, so they'll try to go right over a defender. Ken Willard of the 49ers is a good example. He just bowls over men; he scares them, really. He has defenders psyched. You can see it in the films. He has them ducking or trying to get low so that they don't feel the full impact of him hitting them—and sometimes they don't even hit him. He just keeps on running."

There is another thing many big backs—and even a few smaller ones—do which Kelly thinks is pure foolishness. They sometimes run into a wall of tacklers and refuse to go down until the weight of the wall collapses on them. "I watch some ball carriers fighting long after the issue is closed," says Leroy. "And I know sooner or later that's how they're going to get hurt. There is a time to give that second effort you read so much about, and there is a time to find yourself a soft spot to fall into.

71

"They always said that Jim Taylor was a 'punishing' runner, and that was the reason why he, in turn, got 'punished' by so many hard-hitting tackles. I guess that was just his way. But I think a lot of backs would be better off if they'd learn when to relax after they've been hit and when to keep struggling. A lot of times you get hit and the defenders just hold you up there if you keep struggling. Then other guys come in and hit you late and that's when you can get hurt."

Like Jim Brown, who never suffered a serious injury in pro football, Kelly has a "feel" for when to relax and go down when hit. He, too, has never been seriously hurt while playing for the Browns. Kelly has taken some mind-boggling blows, however, while trying to block. A couple of years ago Cleveland's opening play of a ballgame called for Kelly to block the outside linebacker on a sweep by Ernie Green. On the snap Leroy drove into the linebacker, who welcomed his arrival with a straight right forearm to the head. Kelly went down like a straw scarecrow. He got up, though, and dizzily made his way back to the huddle. Subsequently he carried the ball three times for 12 yards as the Browns drove down to the one-yard line. Quarterback Frank Ryan didn't realize, of course, that Kelly was still woozy. He called an off-tackle play and handed off to Kelly, who ripped over for the touchdown.

When the Browns took possession again, some of the players went to Coach Blanton Collier and told him their star running back was trying to run on rubbery legs. As Leroy started onto the field, Collier grabbed him and sent in a replacement. Kelly sat on the bench, holding an ice pack to his head till the quarter ended. Then he went back in, no longer forced to play on instinct alone.

"The most important thing as far as blocking is concerned," says Kelly, "is the willingness to go and *look* for someone to hit. When you're blocking a large defensive lineman you have to utilize an element of surprise. You're just not big enough to block him one-on-one if he sees you coming. But you can surprise him if you get to him quickly enough—while he's still reading his keys. Say the defensive end is keying on our tackle, watching to see if the tackle blocks down on him. Well, if you can get to him while he's doing this, he may not see you in time to throw you off. This helps the small man against the big guy.

"And when we block, we can't hit him high and try to muscle him. We have to hit him around the knees, where he's most vulnerable. You cut him around the knees because most big men—the ends and tackles and linebackers—don't like to have anyone hitting down there. They actually shy away from you sometimes. So you aim from the waist down and go in hard and fast. But it becomes a little more difficult when you have to go past the line and get a linebacker who's dropped back on pass defense. There's no element of surprise then. They see you coming and they're just waiting to rap you in order to keep you away from their legs."

When it comes to pass-receiving, however, a man like Kelly can get even with the linebackers who bang him around. Then he's usually running short flare patterns to the outside, which the linebackers must cover. Kelly, a former quarterback from Morgan State in Maryland, is an excellent receiver and therefore hard on linebackers who have to try to stay with him.

"The only time I run a pattern on a safety or cornerback is when I'm in an 'up formation' [set close to the line]," says Kelly. "But most of the time they try to isolate me on an outside linebacker, and the fullback runs his patterns on the middle linebacker. We have the option to go inside or outside on the linebacker. If the defense has the linebacker on you by himself, you try to fake him in and go out, or fake him out and go in. The quarterback reads you and the key then is watching the ball into your hands [keeping your eyes right on it]. Of course, you have to see right away what kind of defense the other team's in so that you don't run into an area the defense is rotating into. With more and more defenses rotating to the outside, they're forcing you to go inside, so you can't fake that linebacker too well. The defense tells you what you have to do and then it's up to you to beat it."

This, however, is the kind of challenge Leroy Kelly accepts with quick yet controlled glee. It is hard to believe he was once regarded as too small to be a regular running back in the NFL.

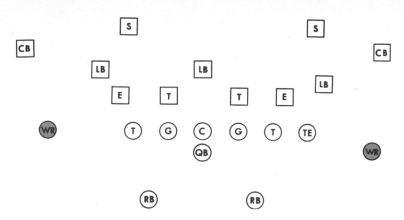

CLIFTON McNEIL
Wide Receiver

In 1968 Clifton McNeil caught 71 passes, leading the National Football League in receiving. But the catch he calls "the most important of my professional career" was the first pass he caught in an exhibition game for the San Francisco 49ers. It set the pace for the fantastic season that was to follow.

During the five seasons he had played for the Cleveland Browns, he had caught exactly 12 passes. Then McNeil asked to be traded to the 49ers. He arrived in California just before San Francisco was to play a preseason game with the Los Angeles Rams, so he had time to get in only one practice session with quarterback John Brodie. As a result, 49er Coach Dick Nolan planned to use McNeil sparingly in the game. He was just going to take a brief look at his new player.

In the second quarter, with the 49ers behind, 14-0, McNeil was sent in. The ball was on the San Francisco 23, and Brodie asked McNeil what kind of pattern he wanted to run. "I didn't know the 49er terminology," Clif recalls, "and John didn't know the Cleveland terminology, so we had to improvise. I told John, 'Let's try that one we did in practice.' I call the play a little hitch-and-go. Bob Hayes [of the Dallas Cowboys] runs the same pattern. He calls it a fly."

McNeil went "burning off the line," stopped short about seven yards out and turned as Brodie pump-faked the pass.

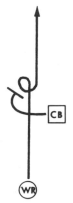

Pass pattern:
Hitch-and-Go

The Ram cornerback lunged up to cover. But McNeil whirled and sped down the sideline. "I hoped to freeze my man," says Clif. "Then I turned on the burner again."

McNeil caught the ball at his 45-yard line—ten yards behind the nearest Ram. From a distance of ten yards, very few people can hope to get anywhere near McNeil—who runs the 100 in 9.5 seconds. The Rams didn't even bother to chase him.

After that, Dick Nolan left McNeil in for the rest of the ballgame. Clif finished with ten catches for the day, catches which gained 196 yards for the 49ers. After five years of frustrating delay, Clifton McNeil's career as an outstanding pro pass receiver had finally begun.

McNeil himself has summarized the basic requirements of his job. "First of all, the basic prerequisites of a wide receiver have always been speed and quickness," says McNeil, who is called "Stick" because he needs only a 28-inch belt around the waist of his six-foot, two-inch body. "But today's wide receiver has to have something else because of the recent great change in defenses from primarily man-to-man to a lot of zone coverage. He must be able to make a fast mental adjustment to the various defenses, which are concealed until the ball is snapped. He must be able to look at the alignment of the defensive backs and linebackers and pick up little signs that tell him what the defense is likely to do on the snap. There are so many defenses today that I think the biggest asset a wide receiver has to have is the ability to read defenses and make a quick mental adjustment. He will then be able to make a quick physical adjustment to them in running his pattern."

Basically, in man-to-man coverage the receiver has only the one defender to beat. In a zone coverage, the wide receiver can shake the cornerback—say, as he cuts to the inside—only to find that a safetyman has picked him up. But if the receiver reads the zone fast enough, he can adjust to defeat the single man who will be covering him in the particular zone the ball is to be thrown in. For example, on a long pass against a given zone, the receiver can forget about the cornerback at a certain

point, knowing full well the cornerback will drop off him and let the safety take him deep.

"I think the cornerbacks these days are better than ever," says Clif. "They all go the 100 in 9.3, 9.4, 9.5 and they're all smart. But they have to play zones now because, in spite of their tremendous ability, I think there are only a couple of them who could play man-to-man against the great wide receivers. I see zone defenses in almost every game now. In a game earlier this season Atlanta used a zone on every single play."

Becoming proficient at reading defenses usually takes some time for even the best receiver. This was one advantage McNeil had during his years of idleness in Cleveland. He had a lot of time in which to study the Browns' regular wide receivers, Paul Warfield and Gary Collins, and he also had plenty of time to study films.

"That's the biggest thing I do now," says Clif, "study films for telltale signs that give the defense away. You can spot a zone sometimes by the alignment of the cornerbacks or the safeties. If the cornerback moves way up close to the line, it often means there's a zone on. Particularly if the man he's playing is one of the real fast receivers. You know that if he wasn't getting extra help from the safety he would be playing back farther.

"With the safeties you watch to see if they're cheating. In a zone coverage the strong safety often has deep responsibility on the flanker. So sometimes he'll move over a step or two closer to the outside. And in a zone the weakside safety often has to come all the way over and cover the tight end, which means he has a lot of ground to cover. So sometimes he'll also cheat a step or two."

In addition to having to make quick adjustments in mid-pattern, the end at times has to be able to make physical adjustments in mid-air in order to get to passes. "You have to change directions with your body in a hurry if your quarterback is rushed into making a bad throw," says Clif. "You may turn for the ball on one side and find it's on the other. You have to be able to swing all the way around and sometimes dive to catch it. . . . You need good hands? Well, I think good hands are mostly a matter of tremendous concentration, period. Despite the fact that you're going to be hit and you know it, despite the fact that your body is exposed as you stretch—you have to be able to blot out everything except looking that ball into your hands. You can't think about or look at anything else except that ball coming into your hands.

"Sometimes we get in trouble when we have what I call a minor distraction. For instance, when you're right at the point of catching the ball and you hear the defender's movements right behind you. If thinking about him makes you take your eyes off the ball, you're going to drop it. This is the classic case of 'hearing footsteps.' A receiver has to have a tremendous sense of feel out there, almost like antennae or radar, to get open and get to the ball. But he's got to blot out all the distractions and concentrate on the ball if he's going to catch it.

"Another distraction to me is when you see a ball that's not ideally thrown. One that seems to be just beyond your range and you know you're going to have trouble catching it. There's a tendency to have a mental letdown and sometimes you give up on the ball. Whenever you let a mental block come between you and the ball, you're in trouble. A receiver must always think positively. Sometimes it's easier to make a diving, one-handed catch if your mind is clear than it is to make an easy catch that's coming right at you, if you're wondering where the defensive back is and maybe starting to run before you've even caught the ball."

All the great receivers have done this at one time or another. It happened to McNeil in 1968 against Baltimore. He ran a "streak"—flat out, no moves—straight down the field against cornerback Bobby Boyd. "I had to be at least five yards ahead of Boyd and everyone else when I turned," says Clif. "The ball was thrown behind me so I had to make an adjustment, but I had plenty of time for it. All I had to do was 'look the ball into my hands,' catch it and run. But because I had to make a mental adjustment to the underthrown pass to coincide with the physical adjustment of coming back for it, I started thinking about the defender back there. (I took for granted that I was going to catch the pass.) In the process I took my eyes off the ball and began to run—and I dropped the pass."

Like most good receivers, McNeil remembers the drops better than the catches. But at the moment the error occurs there is only one thing to do. "You have to strike it from your mind," he says. "You have to discipline yourself to forget it and concentrate on the next one. I often feel that when a receiver's warming up it's sometimes better if he drops a pass instead of catching all of them. You realize what you've done wrong and you start the game with the proper concentration for catching everything that's thrown your way. It sharpens your alertness, and you've got the lapse out of your system."

However, McNeil feels that warm-ups—and every workout with his quarterbacks—are crucial to his performance. They have to be able to read each other precisely, know just what the other is doing at all times. Since every team has two or three quarterbacks, and since no two quarterbacks are exactly alike, receivers must adjust to every passer on their team.

"John Brodie's release is different from Steve Spurrier's," Clif says of his quarterback teammates.

McNeil had good reason for realizing how well he had to know them both when, midway through the 1969 season, Brodie's arm "went dead" and Spurrier became the regular. "Steve's release is much slower than John's, and Steve's passes tend to be softer, so I have to adjust my patterns to him. Say I'm running a hook—straight out and curl back. I can run it deeper if John is throwing because, when I turn, the ball is going to get to me faster—partly because he throws harder and partly because he has a quicker release. His ball is in the air when I'm turning. But with Steve I don't run a hook pattern as deep. He doesn't release as quickly and his throw is a little softer. John has the advantage here with his greater experience."

Because of all the patterns a receiver must run, the amount of time he must spend working with his quarterback is almost unbelievable. And the less natural equipment an end possesses

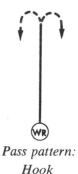

Pass pattern:
Hook

—particularly speed—the more he has to work. Raymond Berry caught more passes for the Colts than any other man had ever caught in pro football history. And he caught them simply because he worked harder than any other end had ever worked. He wasn't fast, but he could run any conceivable pattern so precisely and coordinate his timing with quarterback John Unitas so acutely that Berry was impossible for the defense to cover.

"Most receivers run the same basic patterns," says McNeil. "A post, a flag, a corner, a quick out, a hook, a turn-in, a cross —though different teams have different names for them. A few also run a new pattern that's very effective. I call it a 'burst.' Instead of driving straight up the field, you take three steps in on a 45-degree angle and drive on your man. The angle may vary a little, depending on how your man is playing you. But the burst helps you get a real good alignment on your defensive back. Especially those who hang to the outside on you because they know they're going to get post [inside] help. A lot of cornerbacks just hang out there to the outside and ignore all the moves you make.

"You want your man in a certain position. You want to take something away from him just like he's taking something away from you. That's what I mean by getting good alignment on him. The burst gives him a different look. Now he thinks, 'If this end is coming over to the middle like that, I'd better get over there because I'm four yards away from him and he can catch a hook.' So he moves inside—and that opens up the outside, where the coverage is one-on-one as a rule."

McNeil calls the burst his "secret which I don't like to talk about too much." He learned it in Cleveland with Paul Warfield from end coach Dub Jones and has taught it to the 49ers' fine young end, Gene Washington. But Clif didn't know any other receivers who were running the burst. That was fine with him because the less opposing defenses see of it the slower they will be to counteract it. "I think it's the smoothest, most dangerous initial move you can have," says

Pass pattern:
Flag (toward
goal flag)

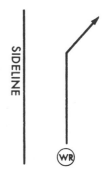

Pass pattern:
Post (toward
goalpost)

81

McNeil. "The defensive back has to make some kind of adjustment to the inside; if he doesn't you'll be free to the inside.

"The burst is also effective against a zone where the halfback is coming up. In most cases the halfback expects you to make an outside release. So the burst can throw him off by making him think you're going inside. In looking at films earlier this season I saw Paul Warfield consistently running a deep-burst-cross against a Washington zone defense and he was open all the time. I think it was due to the element of surprise. He was giving the halfback a different look and freezing the safety, the guy who's supposed to cover deep to the inside. The burst is definitely a good thing to have working for you if you can run it well."

McNeil feels the best cornerback in the NFL is Lem Barney of Detroit, though Clif had pretty good success against him in 1968. A lot of Clif's success had to do with his burst patterns. "I'd been running bursts on him, and then we audibled [changed the play] at the line and I ran a post pattern. Well, Lem has tremendous confidence in himself and he's a gambler. He played me real close and he's *so* quick the ball had to be thrown perfectly. It was. It was just beyond my reach, where I had to stretch way out away from Barney to catch it. He has such good reactions he still went for the ball instead of me. I made the catch and he hit my leg as I turned away. I kept my balance, pulled away and went 65 yards for the touchdown. It was fortunate that I have pretty good range to reach out and catch a ball that would be beyond some other receivers."

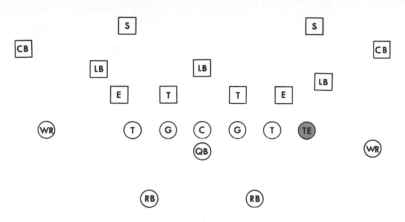

JOHN MACKEY
Tight End

During his rookie season in the National Football League, tight end John Mackey got wide open behind the Los Angeles Rams' secondary. The Baltimore end is extremely fast despite his 220 pounds and his height of six feet, two inches. But the Rams weren't as concerned about the rookie as they were about Baltimore's wide receivers, Raymond Berry and Jimmy Orr. So John was running along by himself, unhindered. The only player on the field who seemed to notice him was Colt quarterback John Unitas, who promptly arched a long pass in his direction. While Mackey was trotting along, looking over his shoulder and waiting for the ball to descend, the Colt bench started cheering. Baltimore was behind, and this sure touchdown would put it ahead.

But just as Mackey reached up for the ball, one of the Rams far behind him yelled, "Look out!"

John's eyes left the ball for a second, and it bounced off his hands. "Everybody who was in the Coliseum that day said the sun got in my eyes when I looked back," Mackey says, smiling. "Heck, I just got fooled by the oldest trick in the world."

John Mackey is not only the finest tight end in the game, he is also probably the most honest. For that reason, when he says, "Next to the quarterback, the most important position on the offensive team is the tight end," you consider his statement

carefully. And it doesn't take long for him to convince you he is right.

"Why?" He repeats your question. "Well, in order to have a good running game, you have to have a tight end who is quick enough to get outside and drive the linebacker in when the play is going around on the big sweep. He has to be big enough to block down on the 270- to 280-pound defensive end. And if the run is up the middle, he must be fast enough to go over and get that middle linebacker. Not many people are aware of how important the tight end is to the running game.

"Now on the passing game," Mackey continues, "because he is in tight next to the tackle, there will be times when he has to stay in and block to help protect the passer. So he has to be practically as big as a lineman himself—yet fast and agile enough to run pass patterns and catch the ball.

"On pass patterns he must be able to release inside—which the strongside linebacker is drilled never to let him do—and to control defenders so that the outside receivers can have one-on-one coverage. Say Willie Richardson is coming from the flanker position on an inside pass pattern. He's the primary receiver. My job is to release inside—get past the linebacker and cut toward the inside of the field. I'm supposed to take the strongside safety, who picks up the tight end in man-to-man coverage, out of the area, and the weakside safety as well, if I can, so that Willie will only have the cornerback to contend with. Now if I stay in and block, the strongside safety will turn out and help double-team on the flanker. If I release after I block for a count or two, my man has to try to pick me up. If

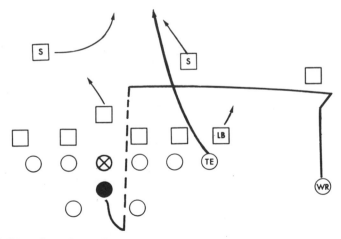

The tight end "splits" the safeties, clearing the middle for a pass to the wide receiver.

he doesn't, if he's back double-teaming, a quarterback like Johnny Unitas will make the adjustment and throw to me. That's what I mean by controlling defenders."

In recent years some teams have been giving the Colts inside-outside, or "split," coverage. That is, the four defensive backs cover lanes. The cornerbacks cover anyone who runs an outside route, and the safeties take anyone who comes to the inside. If Mackey releases inside, then cuts outside, the strongside safety usually stays with him. If John breaks to the outside immediately and the flanker cuts inside, then the strong safety takes Richardson and the cornerback picks up Mackey. But what happens if Mackey runs straight down the middle in the seam between the two safetymen?

"Usually I end up with both of them covering me," says John. "Part of this is due to respect for me and part of it is due to how the defensive team is thinking. If I'm not controlling the safeties, we'll adjust. For instance, as soon as I see I'm not affecting the weakside safety, I'll go back and tell the quarterback, 'I have one-on-one, John, hit me deep.' As soon as I catch one deep going down to the inside, they'll have to respect that. When they respect that, every time I go deep inside, then we have one-on-one on both our outside receivers. See what I mean about controlling?"

John Mackey not only controls defensive backs; he has been known to control entire defenses as well. There was the seven-on-one coverage he received a few years ago against Detroit, for example, but it couldn't stop him. The film has become an NFL classic. The Colts had the ball on the Lion 36 and quarterback Gary Cuozzo, subbing for Unitas, hit Mackey with a five-yard pass on the right side. Cornerback Dick LeBeau drove into him immediately . . . and bounced off. But five other Lions swarmed around Mackey. "There were so many of them," John recalls, "that they were getting in their own way." Mackey started knocking people away with his forearm, which he swings like a scythe. As he burst into the daylight, LeBeau leaped on his back. But John twisted and spun him off, then cut past on-charging tackle Alex Karras. The Colt star went for a 64-yard touchdown. "I had been turned around so many times I was afraid I might be going in the wrong direction," he says, chuckling.

The keys to Mackey's great running ability when he catches the ball are his surprising speed and his lethal forearm. The foot speed is God-given; the forearm action has been developed to ward off tacklers. Trying to arm-tackle him is a waste of time because John simply clubs away one reaching arm. This, in effect, takes away both. Some defensive backs even have a hard time stopping Mackey when they get their shoulders into him, because then he wields that forearm like an uppercut.

"Some of the smaller receivers just go straight down," he says. "But I'm big enough to get away. Besides, if I let them get in the first blow, I'm more likely to get hurt. I don't like getting hurt."

Mackey used his swiftness and clubbing arm to beat the Bears for a 79-yard touchdown a few years ago. He caught a 10-yard pass about eight feet in front of the strongside safety, veteran Richie Petitbon. John knew from experience that Petitbon wouldn't commit himself to making the tackle alone. He would hold his ground, waiting for Mackey to make a move and for help to arrive. So Mackey went right at him, but when he dipped his shoulder as if to make a move he didn't follow through. Instead he drove into Petitbon and brought his right forearm up into his chest, knocking Richie out of his crouch and onto his seat. Then John stiff-armed Dick Butkus as he juked one way and sped past him on the other side. All Mackey had to do then was outrun speedy weakside safety Roosevelt Taylor to the goal line—which he proceeded to do.

Catching passes and then running with the ball seem to be among John Mackey's favorite pastimes on Sundays. But he also loves to block, and the bigger the opponent the better. "I like to block back on the defensive end," he says. "I have an advantage because I have the angle and I know the play. And that end may weigh 280 pounds, so it's really a challenge to hit him. Especially since we block back on the ends so much that lots of times they're just waiting in anticipation. That makes it fun. But I know what I'm doing and I know where the play is going. It's up to the end to figure it out. While he's figuring it out, I have the advantage."

The secret is to hit first and get into that end before he has read the play. This, as far as John Mackey is concerned, is what blocking's all about. You ask him to tick off the ideal physical requirements of a tight end and he says, "I would want a guy about six-three who can run the hundred in nine seconds flat." When he stops laughing, he says, "Seriously, he must be strong enough to block the big ends so I'd want him to have some size, say at least a height of six-three. But weight just doesn't mean that much. I've always felt that quickness is much more important than weight. Even though you may be smaller, if you hit a man hard enough before he starts moving, you can move him. I think weight has a tendancy to make a man sluggish. So I would want a tall, slim tight end who was very quick.

"And I would also want a tight end who was smart enough to make adjustments quickly, because this game is a game of adjustments. Things don't really start happening until the ball is snapped. That's when you have to read the defense and react to it. So the tight end must be able to read the defense quickly. Is it man-to-man, inside-outside, a zone, or whatever? And he must also know what all of his other pass receivers are doing or will do against that particular defense. And, of course, he has to be able to block like a lineman and catch the ball. I consider the tight end a lineman who can run pass patterns and catch the ball."

Mackey feels fortunate to have signed with the Baltimore Colts because they have always been a passing team and they have always had a great quarterback in Johnny Unitas. "I came into pro football playing with 'J. U.'," says Mackey, "and J. U. is the best. I think our passing game is the best also.

We work on it an awful lot, and this is important to a tight end. You talk to some other tight ends and maybe they won't stress the timing between them and the quarterback or the ability to catch the ball or some of the other things I've stressed as a receiver. I feel this way because I play for the Colts, and this is how the Colts have always used their tight ends. We pass a lot so we need everyone to be able to receive. Green Bay, on the other hand, likes to run a lot. So they want a big, tough tight end who can really block.

"You look around and you'll see a number of teams who use their tight ends mainly as blockers. Occasionally they'll be used as receivers of short passes. For a long time Dallas tight ends never caught a lot of passes, but they were usually very strong blockers. You'd seldom see a pass to a Dallas tight end on third-and-ten or on any other possession play. They were used as decoys."

Sometimes the team sets the style of its tight end's play, and sometimes the tight end himself sets the style of his own play. After the Cowboys acquired Mike Ditka—who is not only a fine blocker but a fine receiver as well—they began to throw to their tight end more. "Some tight ends are very strong and not very fast," says John, "like Billy Truax of the Rams. And others are very fast but not great blockers, like Pete Retzlaff when he played with the Eagles."

The Colts were certain Mackey was going to be an outstanding all-round tight end when they saw him play the position at Syracuse. He caught few passes because they seldom threw passes at Syracuse, but his skills were self-evident. John became Baltimore's top draft choice in 1963. He reported to training camp and found himself not only the biggest but also the fastest end on the Colts.

His main problems initially were catching low passes and reading defenses. Johnny Unitas suggested he lose a couple of inches around his waist so that he could bend over easier to get under low-thrown balls. John lost a couple of inches off his waist and began scraping balls off the grass. The recognition of defenses, however, took a bit longer.

"I can remember being afraid that I didn't know what I was doing that first year," John recalls. "I knew exactly what I had to do in any given situation—in practice. I studied hard and knew what to do. But there are certain adjustments you have to make that come only after you've played pro ball for a while. So when the defense would show me something I hadn't seen in practice, I didn't know what to do. Naturally, it made me feel uncomfortable. But when they'd show me something new, I'd come back to the huddle and tell Unitas that I didn't know who to block on that play, and we could easily find out how to adjust from the sidelines."

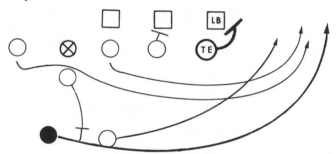

On a sweep the tight end must block the linebacker to the inside.

One other problem he had as a rookie was the block that every tight end—veteran or rookie—has the most trouble with. "Trying to hook the linebacker [drive him in on a sweep] when he's set outside of you. Now, as I've said, blocking back on the defensive end is simply a matter of getting up on the count and hitting him first. But when the linebacker is outside of me and has outside responsibilities on the play . . . well, it's tough.

"Dave Robinson of Green Bay is particularly hard to hook, and so is Dave Wilcox of the San Francisco 49ers. They're so strong that, when I have to try to hook them, we sort of have a stalemate on the line of scrimmage. I don't really knock them down, but I'm in their way and I've tied them up so that we just might get around that corner at times. At other times I have to just go on and take them to the outside and hope that our back can cut back to the inside. When you're dealing with a linebacker who has been taught not to get hooked, it's very, very hard to hook him."

Occasionally you'll notice the tight end-linebacker stalemate in ballgames. The end is digging as hard as he can, trying to turn the big backer, who is clubbing away at him. And the unfortunate ball carrier, approaching the impasse, is not really sure whether to swing outside or turn it up inside.

"That's the kind of thing that breaks me up when we watch the cartoons [films of the previous game] on Tuesday morning," Mackey says through a smile. "You sit there and you watch your performance and you can see some pretty wild things . . . a block you tried to throw and missed . . . a play where you were loafing when you thought you were hustling . . . a time you thought you hit a guy real hard when you were really only pussyfooting. The coaches are deadly serious about it, of course, but among themselves the players do a lot of hazing. If I miss a block someone might say, 'Oh man, I guess age is creeping up on you,' or 'You sure didn't look like an All-Pro there.' "

But fortunately for the Baltimore Colts, at least 90 percent of the time John Mackey, tight end, looks very much like an All-Pro.

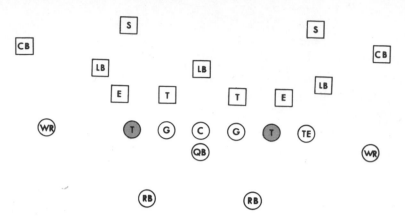

BOB BROWN
Offensive Tackle

The weight room of the Rams was empty except for offensive tackle Bob Brown, who tends to make the place a second home. With his height of six feet, four-and-a-half inches, and weight of 278 pounds, Bob seemed to fill the room. Although Brown lifts weights daily, his muscles aren't rounded like those of the average weight lifter. Instead, they are knotty, like the muscles in the backs and chests of men who work on the docks. His 55-inch chest looks as if you'd need a clothesline to measure it.

Brown has had awesome strength ever since he came into the National Football League in 1964 as a number one draft choice out of the University of Nebraska. An All-league performer for years, he has been voted the outstanding blocker in the NFL in a national poll conducted by the 1,000-yard club. Consequently you can't help wondering why he keeps straining so hard with the weights. What makes him continue to drive himself to train all year round? If you remember something he said at the Philadelphia Eagles' training camp a few years ago, it may help you to better understand his fanatical drive.

"When I was a kid in Cleveland," Brown explained, "we played that old game King of the Hill. You did anything to get on top. You scratched, kicked, punched, bit, put a

thumb in the other guy's eye . . . I mean anything to get on top. Once I got on top, I made up my mind I was going to stay up there. Nobody was going to move me. It's the same way with pro football. Right now I'm King of the Hill—and that's the way it's going to be until the day I quit."

When you come right down to it, this is what makes Bob Brown the best offensive tackle in professional football. But beyond the basic factors of his size, agility and speed and that fantastic desire to stay on top is his unique style of play.

"The responsibilities of the job are relatively simple," says Brown, who speaks in a surprisingly soft, gentle voice. "You keep the defensive end off the passer in a passing situation, and on running plays you get the ball carrier room to run. My personal philosophy on how to accomplish this is somewhat different from most offensive tackles. My game is based on an attack formula. I like to attack constantly from the whistle to the gun. By doing this, I believe I can wear down the defensive end. Consequently, during the third and fourth quarters, he's not coming on nearly as strong as he was during the early part of the game.

"Most tackles do it differently. As a rule they play with a little more finesse, just trying to screen the defensive end away from the quarterback. By screening on a pass block, you just kind of run along with the guy, trying to stay between him and the quarterback. You bump him and run along, bump him and run along, bump him and run along, giving ground but always turning him away from your passer.

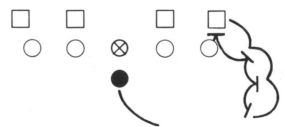

The tackle's pass block.

"Now instead of simply taking the blow from the defensive end, I try to punish him," says Brown. As the tackle's heavy, black brows knit together in a menacing frown, the interviewer is thankful he's not a defensive end.

"Instead of being a shock absorber, I'm the one who is transmitting the shock. I unload on them. I like to compare my style to a sledge hammer. It's not fancy, it's crude-looking, but it works. I don't try to hit the shoulder pads or anything else that's padded. I like to go after the soft spots underneath the pads. I like to hit spots that are tender, that I know are sensitive and consequently transmit a considerable amount of pain. I don't know of any other tackles who approach the game this way."

Brown's hard-hitting style comes as quite a shock to defensive ends who are used to using offensive tackles as blocking dummies on pass plays. The ends smash the tackles and try to get them off balance so they can throw them aside with their hands and dash into the quarterback. Or the ends try to fake around the tackle who is dropping back. Brown drives into them on every play, whether it be a pass or a run. And it hurts. As the game progresses, it hurts more and more. The bruises widen and deepen.

"I use a two-hand rip-up on both pass blocks and run blocks," Bob says. "I block more with my hands than with my shoulders because, as I said, I'm working on soft spots. Hitting a player's pads means nothing. It sounds good and the fans and coaches like to hear it. But I don't think I'm accomplishing my purpose when I do that.

"Regardless of who the individual is, I think the universal quotient for this particular occupation is pain. And regardless of who I'm playing against, if I apply enough pain I can break the guy down. This is how I approach the game—applying pain constantly. When I think I've got a guy in trouble, I apply pain in the area where I think I'm hurting him most. I just keep gnawing away at that spot because I know eventually I'm going to wear him down and he's going to slow down."

A man who deals in pain must know how to cope with it himself. Before the final exhibition game at the beginning of the 1969 season, Bob's hamstring muscles were so sore that he could hardly walk and his right arm ached so badly that he could barely get it up to comb his hair. But when it came to the opening game against the Colts, he told Ram trainer

George Menefee, "I don't care much about exhibitions, but when we play the Colts, if you got enough Novocaine, I'll play." True to his word, Brown took a shot of Novocaine in his arm and then went out against six-foot, seven-inch, 295-pound Baltimore defensive end Bubba Smith. Smith had just come off an exhibition performance against the Dallas Cowboys. In that game he had run all over Ralph Neely, one of the best offensive tackles in pro football. But against the Rams, Bubba was nowhere to be seen in the Ram backfield.

"Bubba comes well, he comes real well, but I had a good day," says Bob Brown, who has too much respect for his opponents to put down individual players. "That game was the highlight of my career up to now. At Philadelphia, I had played the Colts, oh, probably six or seven times in regular- and exhibition-season games, and we never beat them. When you defeat a team that has Johnny Unitas, John Mackey and Jimmy Orr and Rick Volk, Bob Vogel and all those others, that's tremendous to me. It means a hell of a lot because you beat the best. No, I didn't say anything to Bubba out there that day. It's just like an assembly line. You do your job and go home."

The job that offensive tackles dislike most is pass-blocking. Again, this is because they are not aggressors on pass-blocking. They stand there and get smacked around. Brown would rather pass-block than do anything else. On running plays, the defensive end is often moving away from him and thus it is difficult to hit a clean shot.

"But on pass blocks I'm just sitting there waiting for that defensive end," says Brown, his mustache lifting at the ends in a slight smile. "He has to come to me because he's got to get by me in order to get to the quarterback. I know it and he knows it and it makes his job tough. You see, I come to smoke and I'm going to burn from the time the whistle blows until the man in the striped shirt shoots that little .22 he's got in his back pocket. I'm beating away at that end all afternoon, and he's got to try to come *through* me.

"Now when I set up, what I do is take something away from him, either the inside or the outside. I set up to one side or the other so he's only got one side he can possibly take on me. If I do that, I know the only way he can go to beat me and I'm ready for it. That makes my job easy.

"Some of these guys try to get you with the head fakes and jukes. But I don't ever take that stuff. Sometimes I may stick them quick, but usually I just sit there and watch them juke around. You don't have to take those fakes because ultimately he's got to come through you. So you get your initial position and just sit there and wait. The whole thing is, if you take these head fakes, you're hurting yourself because then you're giving him two ways to go on you and you're liable to throw yourself off balance. So I wait, and when he finally comes I attack with my two-hand rip-up.

"And, again, this attacking on pass-blocking helps set up my blocking for the running game, too. If I were finessing him all day he'd be better able to fight me off on runs. But if I'm physically hurting him on pass blocks, he's just not as well equipped physically to keep me off him on runs."

With his speed and quickness, Brown can be a key blocker on sweeps to the opposite side of the line. This is something many big tackles just can't execute fast enough. He is also excellent on difficult cut-off blocks to the opposite side. On a cut-off block, he has to get across the line and into a linebacker almost before the ball is snapped. Otherwise the linebacker has slid across into the play. Then the offensive tackle, when hitting him, only tends to drive the linebacker farther into the runner.

"There is one play, however, that Brown—as well as every other offensive tackle in the League—admits he has trouble with. "Trying to hook a defensive end to the inside when the play is supposed to go to the outside," says Bob. "First of all, the end's lined up on your outside shoulder. Sometimes he'll even cheat over a step or so when he wants to make a strong outside rush. If a sweep is called at this time, you can forget about hooking him to the inside. It's hard enough when he's set in his regular position outside your shoulder. He's been trained and indoctrinated not to be hooked. So when I start out to hook him he takes a lateral step to the outside, and we can keep going like that all the way to the sideline. That is all you can do—keep driving him as fast as you can and hope you don't jam up the sweep. Of course, if everyone else blocks well, your halfback can turn upfield right inside the end, right off my tail. Then we can still get a good gain out of the play."

Brown started playing pro ball with the Philadelphia Eagles, but he is happy he was traded to the Rams. First of all, they are consistently contenders. The second reason is more personal—he no longer has to face unhookable Deacon Jones. "He is undoubtedly the greatest defensive end ever to play this game," says Bob. "You cannot—it's impossible, absolutely impossible—hook him. He's strong against the blast block. He's faster than most backs, and he has more quickness than you would believe. He just beats you to death with his quickness, never with sheer strength.

"My most frustrating experience as a pro was my first meeting with Deacon when I was a rookie. He'd give me the inside move and I'd take it because I was a rookie. Then he'd go outside and beat me. I started thinking, 'What the heck is the guy doing?' He'd go inside, then outside, then inside again. He beat me every way you can. He wasn't hurting me physically and that was even more frustrating. I was constantly wondering what I could do to stop him. And remember, you only have 25 seconds between plays to make your adjustments, so you're constantly thinking what to try next. I just kept hoping that one time he'd come right to me so I could bring some smoke to him. But he never gave me that shot. Pure frustration."

Having been an offensive guard at Nebraska, the transition to tackle in the pros required a considerable adjustment for Bob Brown. When you play guard, the defensive tackle is lined up right in front of your nose. At tackle, the other team's defensive end is set outside of you and he can move around to take different angles charging in. It is more difficult for the offensive lineman to get a solid shot at an end than at a tackle. But Brown learned and he's still learning.

Beyond his primary technique of blasting away on every play to wear down his opponent, Bob Brown uses a number of tricks to beat defensive ends. They are really a very small part of his game, as you notice when you see him play. Most of the time you see "big number 76" driving into his man, his huge neck hunched into his shoulders, his massive forearms out like wings, his size 13 cleats throwing bits of grass and earth behind his short, choppy steps. He doesn't talk about his tricks but occasionally you'll notice one. Such as in that opening game against the Colts.

Brown was sticking Bubba Smith all afternoon. On one play Bob drove into Bubba, then dropped back quickly in a pass-blocking stance. Brown hit him again. Bubba bounced and charged once more. Suddenly Brown threw himself across Smith's legs, knowing full well the tall Colt end would leap over him and dash toward Ram quarterback Roman Gabriel. Just as Smith got to Gabriel, the quarterback was throwing a screen pass to halfback Les Josephson. Josephson not only had two guards in front of him but by this time Bob Brown was there as well. The play went for a seven-yard gain and would have gone for more except for an exceptional play by Colt linebacker Mike Curtis.

Just as Bob Brown doesn't talk about how he occasionally makes use of deception on a football field, neither does he talk about outstanding plays he has made. "Does an accountant come home bragging that he just found a great new way to beat the government on taxes? No. I'm always trying to do the best job humanly possible and that's why I can't isolate any particular instance and say, 'This day I did a great job.' Every time I go out there I'm trying to give the people their money's worth. Then when it's over I try to forget it.

"That's also why a lot of publicity doesn't mean that much

to me. Press clippings and trophies are nice to show off in the den, but it all comes down to one thing—top tackles get top dollars. The thing that makes Bob Brown go is the money."

That and the desire to remain King of the Hill.

Bob Brown excused himself and began his daily ritual of lifting weights. "It adds to my strength and it also gives me a psychological edge that I feel I need," he said. "I *feel* stronger than my man." It may well be that the feeling is mutual.

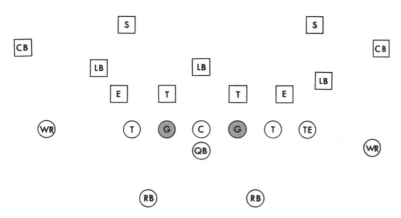

GALE GILLINGHAM
Offensive Guard

The Packers were wearing the gray sweat suits they use in practice. (The defensive players had red vests over their shirts to set them apart.) Quarterback Bart Starr called signals, took the snap and dropped back to pass. It was the last play of the workout and defensive tackle Henry Jordan tried to get around guard Gale Gillingham with quick moves, but Gillingham did not hit and give ground, hit and give ground the way most guards do when pass-blocking. Instead, he stepped into Jordan and pretty much held his ground—his muscle and weight planted solid.

Later, as Gillingham walked off the field, he talked about the rigors of being a guard in professional football. "Yes, there are different styles of playing the position," said the 6-foot-3 Gale, whose 255-pound frame seems even broader through the chest and shoulders when seen from close up. "The style has to fit your body. For example, Forrest Gregg played guard a lot differently than I do. He was more of a finesser. Gregg never did anything the same way twice in a row."

One of the finest offensive tackles in the league, Gregg had to fill in at guard for several long stretches because of injuries to other Packer linemen. What Gregg and most pro football guards tend to do is change-up consistently in order to keep the defensive tackles they face off balance. This is particularly true on pass protection, where in the mind of many defensive tackles the guard is just a big punching bag blocking his path to the quarterback. The tackles weigh between 250 and 300 pounds and they come at the guards with everything they have. A forearm swings to the jaw or stomach, a padded hand slaps against the ear hole of the helmet, causing the brain to reverberate. A pair of hands grasps the shoulder guards and yanks the blocker out of the way. Or maybe the powerful tackle simply attempts to run right over the smaller man.

"Guards like Gregg feel the best way they can do the job is to keep the tackles guessing," says Gillingham. "And Forrest was real good at that. One time he'd go at the tackle aggressively, and really fire into him. The next time he'd back off right away, then pop the tackle. He relied on quickness and changing-up. I try to use my size more. Because I'm a little bit bigger than most guards, I use strength a little more. Basically I just try to overpower my man."

Gillingham does not mean that he uses his size and strength more aggressively. It's just the opposite. He does not fire out, hit, recover, then fire again as other guards do in protecting their quarterback.

"That method is more aggressive than the way I do it," says Gale, "but there is more of a chance of the man's getting around you. I try to set up and catch the guy coming in. Then I sort of tie him up right there. If the smaller guard tried to do this, he would probably just be overpowered. I try to get up into the face of the tackle and stay there, where the smaller guys have to worry about getting driven back. I try to get my helmet up under the tackle's chin and ride him. You have to be big enough to do that, but it's worked out as a good technique for me. You don't want the tackle to penetrate. That's almost as bad as letting him get to your quarterback. You see, after the tackle penetrates a few yards, he can put his hands up and your quarterback can't see the receivers."

Although Gillingham was a two-way tackle at the Univer-

Ed. VeBell

sity of Minnesota, he actually played more defense than offense. But as one of Green Bay's number one draft choices in 1966, he was immediately turned into an offensive guard. He found pass-blocking the most difficult transition to the pros. "In college you just didn't do that much pass-blocking," says

Gilly, as he is called by his teammates. "You drove your guy back three yards and a ball carrier would go through for three yards. Here you may move your man a half a yard and then you turn him or shield him—just stay in his face. The guy who keeps his feet is the guy who's going to win."

Gillingham feels it's equally important for a successful pro guard to keep his head. First of all, a blocker can't lose his temper when a big defensive tackle rams a hand up under his face mask. If the guard lashes out in retaliation, it's going to cost his team 15 yards. The guard may even be thrown out of the ballgame for fighting. Secondly, the guard can't let himself get rattled if he is outplayed. When that happens too frequently, even the best ballplayers have a tendency to get shaken. Once they do, there is a very good chance that they'll forget all their technique. Then, of course, their game gets worse and worse. Thirdly, a guard has to keep his head if he expects to be able to think and react under tremendous pressure. A defense can suddenly show the guard something entirely new—for example, an odd-man line with the tackles and ends looping and the linebackers blitzing. If the defensive team has never used that before, the guard is not expecting it. He has to react instantly to handling a different man—the end —who is coming at him from a different angle.

The physical requirements of the position are awesome, too. "You have to be fast enough and agile enough to pull out of the line and lead your halfbacks and fullbacks down the field," says Gilly. (Gale himself has been timed at 5.8 seconds for 50 yards, a speed many linebackers would not be ashamed of.) "You also have to be able to handle the guy ahead of you on traps or runs up the middle—either drive him back or cut him off to open a hole. You've got to be quick enough at times to plunge out there and get that middle linebacker, too. And on plays to the other side you've got to be able to neutralize your man, then go across the field and handle someone else.

"So, along with speed and agility, you have to have enough size to stand in there and pass-block against tackles like Merlin Olsen (six feet, five inches tall, 275 pounds), Roger Brown (six feet, five inches tall, 300 pounds) and Bob Lilly (six feet, five inches tall, 260 pounds). This is the toughest and most critical job for a guard because, as I said, if you don't keep your guy out, he's liable to put your quarterback out, or at least knock the ball down. The thing that makes it so tough, of course, is that you can't use your hands and the other guy can. He comes blowing in there with all that momentum and he can use his hands to throw you right out of the way. But you have to be sure to keep your hands in close to your chest or the officials can call you for holding, which is 15 yards."

Gillingham was fortunate to have practiced for years against one of the best defensive tackles in the game, Henry Jordan. Jordan made up for lack of size by his extreme quickness. He was very difficult to get a solid hit on. He was what Gilly calls "a dancer," a guy who fakes one way, then the other way, and slips past the guard on the original side. Tackles like Jordan, Alex Karras of the Lions and Bob Lilly of the Cowboys are so agile they have been known to get past the guard without even being touched.

"I'll never forget the first game I started," Gilly recalls. "Fuzzy Thurston was out with an injury during my rookie year [1966] and we were going into Baltimore. We had to win that game because the conference title depended upon it. I have to admit I was scared. I was worried about letting the team down because I was going up against Billy Ray Smith, who is so quick he's called 'Rabbit.' He's a lot like Jordan in that he jumps around a lot. He gives you a move to try to draw you forward and then goes the other way. But because I had practiced against Henry all week, I was ready for him. I wasn't any great shakes, but I had a fairly decent game. And the fact that we won with me in there made me feel like a real part of the team even though I was only a rookie."

The Packers scored first in that game and kept scoring, which took the pressure off the offensive line. The Baltimore defensive line had to worry about both the run and the pass, since Green Bay was moving the ball with equal ease both in the air and on the ground. But when your team falls behind, it's a different story for the offensive linemen. Then the rush line can be fairly certain the offense will be throwing the football to try and catch up. When a rush line knows there is a good chance that the next play will be a pass, it can virtually ignore the run and simply tee off on the offensive linemen, coming flat out on the snap.

This is what happened in the first game of the 1967 season, when the Packers met the Lions in Green Bay. "I guess that was the worst game I ever had," says Gilly, who was a regular by that time. "It was our opener and we got up too early. We all got nervous and excited and fell behind. The Lions started off by recovering an on-side kick, scored and went ahead by 17-0 at halftime. In the second half we were just throwing the football, and they were coming on every play. I was playing against Jerry Rush that day, and it was about the longest game I can ever remember."

Jerry Rush wasn't the only Lion tackle who put the pressure —and often the complete body—on Green Bay's quarterback Bart Starr. Time after time Alex Karras seemed to be past Green Bay guard Jerry Kramer before the Packers' veteran All-league performer got out of his set position. Green Bay was happy to settle for a 17-17 tie in that game. In the second meeting of the season between the Packers and Lions, however, both Gillingham and Kramer played outstanding games, and Green Bay won. The Packers did not fall behind, so there was no undue pressure on the Green Bay offensive linemen.

Although Jerry Rush is not among the All-league defensive tackles, he managed to give Gillingham a very difficult time in more than one ballgame. A tackle who gave Gilly a very difficult time in every game they played together was Dallas' Bob Lilly. Gillingham was just as pleased when he was switched from left guard to right guard, because then he no longer had to battle Lilly.

"Lilly was by far the toughest for me," says Gale. "He is

very big, very agile and very quick. As I said, some tackles are dancers, some like to grab you by the shoulder pads and pull you to one side so they can go around you, and some like to try to run over you. These are the basic moves of various individuals. Well, Lilly combines all of them and adds a few more of his own.

"I remember the 1967 NFL championship game at Green Bay—the game they called the Ice Bowl. I had a pretty good first half against Lilly, but by the time we came out for the second half the field had frozen. It wasn't supposed to, of course. As you may remember, they had those electric heating wires buried under the turf and they were supposed to keep the field from freezing. But I think the heating system failed when the temperature dropped to around five degrees below zero.

"Well, when we came out for the second half, all of the Packers were still wearing regular football shoes. But some of the Dallas linemen—including Lilly—had changed into a sort of soccer type shoe. He started going around me so easily I couldn't believe it. I was just skating around trying to make contact with him.

"At first our center, Ken Bowman, and I couldn't figure out what was wrong. Why did Lilly and the other Dallas linemen have such superior footing when we were waltzing around so unsteadily we could hardly stand up? Then we noticed their shoes, and the light dawned. Fortunately, Bowman managed to pick up Lilly when he got by me during most of the last two quarters. But even with Ken to bail me out I thought that that second half would never end."

After two running plays to the other side had failed near the goal line, Green Bay won the game, only because Bart Starr called a quarterback sneak over Jerry Kramer. And Kramer just happened to be standing in the only yard of turf at Lambeau field that hadn't frozen solid. He got some traction and was able to move the skidding Dallas tackle, Jethro Pugh, back far enough for Starr to slide in for the winning score.

Gillingham has patterned much of his playing style after

Jerry Kramer, now retired. "He was one of the best," says Gilly, "as was Fuzzy Thurston, who was smaller but knew how to handle guys from all his experience. . . . Who are some of the other exceptional guards? Well, Howard Mudd of the Chicago Bears is excellent. He's another big guard. He has exceptional balance and good all-around technique. Gene Hickerson of the Cleveland Browns is a smaller guard who is also excellent. His assets are his quickness and agility. Cleveland runs more pitch-out plays than we do, which means its guards have to pull even quicker than we do.

"A lot of people don't realize just how quick a guard must be on wide plays, pitch-outs or sweeps. If you can't get out in front of the running backs, you can't play in the NFL. This is particularly true with the Packers, because we pull our guards as much as any team in the League—maybe even more. You know the Lombardi Sweep that Lombardi made famous with Kramer and Thurston pulling for Hornung and Taylor? It's still a key play for us, and a young guard coming in had better have that basic speed when he gets here. You have to be able to get off the ball quick without tipping off the play beforehand by leaning back or anything else. And you've got to be able to

On a sweep the guards "pull" out of the line to lead the ball-carrier.

think on the run because we have a lot of option plays. You may have to turn in if, say, the defensive end and linebacker slide outside too fast, or you may have to go around if they stay in. You have to make a decision in a hurry because the back is right on your tail following you."

And it would be very embarrassing for a great big fellow to be run over by a small man wearing the same uniform and carrying a football!

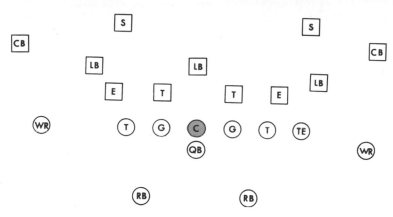

MICK TINGELHOFF
Center

Henry Michael Tingelhoff of the Minnesota Vikings, veteran All-league center, wears the badge of his profession on his forehead. During the playing season, the badge is a nasty gash; in the off-season it is a bump of calcium deposits that have built up over the years. The gash and bump are the result of his helmet's banging down on his forehead when he drives his helmet into the chests of his huge opponents. This badge is the occupational hazard of smaller linemen throughout football, because the only way they can deal with the monsters they must face is to use this "spear method." For a helmet in the gut is equal to 20 or more pounds on the opponent's body.

"Most centers aren't as big as the other offensive linemen," says Tingelhoff, who stands 6-1 and weighs 237 pounds. "They usually range, oh, from 230 to 245 pounds. So the center has to be kind of a unique combination of strength and speed. Most of us just aren't big enough to overpower the middle linebackers or defensive tackles. What I try to do is drive my head into his chest and then bring my helmet up to get him under the chin. Against some of the real strong middle linebackers like Ray Nitschke of the Packers or Dick Butkus of the Bears, I'll fire out on him and hit him high early in the game, spear him good a few times. Then I'll change-up. I'll fire out as if I'm gonna hit him high. By the time I get to him he's

braced, just waiting for me. Then I'll hit him with a cross-body block about knee high. That's usually effective. I don't mean I always *handle* them, but I usually tie them up so they don't have time to see where the ball carrier is going and chase after him."

110

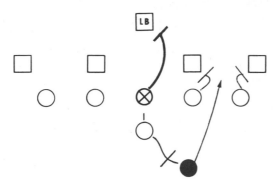

On an off-tackle play the center must block the middle linebacker away from the direction of play.

Basically, the center has to block the middle linebacker on all straight-ahead running plays—either up the middle or off tackle—where the middle backer is directly in front of him. The center has to block the defensive tackle on quick traps up the middle or on end sweeps. And on pass plays the center has to pick up anybody who comes through on a blitz on one side. (A running back is responsible for the other side.) If there is no blitz, the center picks up any rush lineman who gets past the offensive guards or tackles. This is called "option block-ing," taking the first man through and "sticking him."

"It is probably the thing I do best," Tingelhoff says of his pass-blocking. "And of course it's very important. If you don't pick up the blitzers, your quarterback usually doesn't com-plete the pass. Since the middle linebacker is normally right in front of the center, you have to be very quick in snapping the ball, backing up and watching where the middle linebacker goes. If he's coming right on that snap, you'd better be back there in a hurry and in position to block him. It's not always the middle linebacker who's blitzing, either. It could be one of the outside linebackers, or even a defensive back. So you do have to set up quickly.

"You also have to be quick blocking the middle linebacker on running plays. They're all big and fast and smart and they just don't miss making the tackle if they have a shot at the run-ner. Some linebackers are extremely quick and agile, and they don't like to stay in one spot. They move around so much it's hard to get into them. Others prefer to wait, find out where the ball is, then go. As I said, I'm not very big so I can't stick them all the time. With the real strong ones, I have to try to cut their feet from under them. Some of the bigger centers, like Jim Otto of the Oakland Raiders, are strong enough to take on the linebackers up top and drive them back. If the linebacker's not too strong, I will try to overpower him, too. Then I'll change-up, fake coming high and hit him low. I can't go after any of them the same way too many times in succession."

Mick feels that if he gets to any middle linebacker's lower body or knees, he's got a pretty good chance of controlling him. Unfortunately all the middle linebackers have enormous forearms, which they swing like nightsticks all over the center's head. That tends to keep the blockers off.

"The linebacker raps you in the head every time you come out at him," says Mick. "They're just standing there, and they've got that forearm all padded up. It feels like a chunk of concrete smacking into your head. They really use those fore-arms to keep you from getting into them."

Even more difficult to move out than the linebackers are the defensive tackles, several of whom weigh over 300 pounds. Mick tries to hit them right around the midsection with his shoulder. He knows the play, the snap count and he has the angle. This gives him a chance to get into the tackle—who is not back a couple of yards like the middle backer—before the big man can move. Tingelhoff puts his head on one side of the tackle or the other, depending on where the runner is supposed to go, and drives as hard as he can.

"You have to stay away from their upper bodies where they're so strong," Mick says. "Tackles like Bob Lilly of the Dallas Cowboys, Alex Karras of the Detroit Lions and Merlin Olsen and Roger Brown of the Los Angeles Rams are all out-standing. They not only have size, they have great quickness. They come off the ball low and hard, and they read our offensive plays very well. To get a defensive tackle, a center must fire out and quickly try to beat him to the punch with good position, good technique and good leg drive."

The toughest play for Tingelhoff is the one where a big tackle lines up right over him on a pass rush. Not because the tackle tries to run over him—since most of them don't—but because the tackle bats him around so hard with his hands.

"They slap you to one side and go to the other to try to get around you," he says. "They're so big and quick and they slap you so hard that it's murder to try to slow them up. They're supposed to have their hands open when they slap you," he chuckles, "but once in a while . . ."

Most fans don't realize it, but the center has to be one of the most intelligent men on a team. He is the quarterback of the offensive line and often changes the blocking assignments when the teams line up. He sees the defense in a formation that will not permit the normal blocking assignments to work and he makes a code-word call that tells everyone up front what to do.

Suppose Tingelhoff comes up to the line on an off-tackle play where he's supposed to hit the middle linebacker. There's no way he can do it if the tackle has moved over directly in front of him. Mick can call out something like, "George," which means he will take the tackle. The Viking guard, whose tackle has shifted over in front of the center, will then go out and get the middle linebacker.

"On a sweep, for instance, both of our guards are pulling and I am responsible for either the middle linebacker or the onside tackle [The onside being the side to which the sweep is going]. Now, if I want to take the middle linebacker, I'll make the call and *my* onside tackle will come down on their defensive tackle. But if the middle linebacker is shading over to the side we're sweeping, and I don't think I can get him, I'll call a signal where I tell my tackle I'm going after the defensive tackle. That means he has to take the linebacker.

"So a center must be smart; he must know defenses and his own offense real well," says Tingelhoff. "A real good center who makes great blocking calls can really help the offensive guards and tackles because he helps them get good blocking angles. On all the plays up the middle, we have two or three variations of blocking assignments, depending on how the defense lines up. What they show me determines how I want my guards and myself to block. There are a lot of plays that simply *require* a call. You have to make a change if the play is going to work. And there are a lot of other plays where you don't *have* to make a call, but if you see something in the defense that will improve your blocking angles even a little bit, then you want somebody to make a call."

The center's blocking changes are all-important on pass plays, too. In the opening game of the 1969 season, for example, Viking quarterback Gary Cuozzo made an unorthodox "audible" call that went for a touchdown simply because of his confidence in Tingelhoff's ability to read a defense and make the proper blocking changes. The Giants had two linebackers and their weakside safetyman blitzing. Cuozzo read it when he stepped to the line behind Tingelhoff. Gary called an automatic. Mick supported him by making a blocking call that would assign a man to handle each of the blitzers. Instead of the usual pass on a blitz—the quick down-and-in—Cuozzo sent wide end Gene Washington on a fly pattern. Of course it takes some time for a man to get open on a fly, and very few teams would attempt such a play if they knew a three-man blitz was on.

Giant cornerbacker Willie Williams, who was beaten for the 48-yard touchdown on the play, said afterward, "On a blitz you can count the teams on one finger who go for the bomb. Hell, Joe Namath has as good an arm as there is in football but when he reads a blitz he goes for the down-and-in pass. I tell you, that Mick Tingelhoff, he's the best center in the league. He read that blitz, too, and changed all the blocking assignments for the linemen. That's how they picked up all our blitzers and why the play went."

Tingelhoff takes great satisfaction in making the right call at the right time. But personally what he digs most is really popping somebody man-to-man. "I really enjoy getting a good hit on somebody, whether it be a linebacker or a lineman," Mick says, smiling. "You know, really bouncing his head back. I think I get as much pleasure from that as a back would from a long run, or an end would from making a big catch.

"I especially love hitting a blitzing linebacker and really knocking him down or snapping his head back. Real early in my career Joe Schmidt, who was probably one of the finest middle linebackers ever to play this game, blitzed one time and he never saw me. I got a real good hit on him—I mean I really creamed him. It made me feel good. He didn't say anything except, 'Real good hit.' There's not much talking out there. Of course, I've been dropped pretty good a few times, too."

He can take a bruising beating from the big tackles when he's snapping the ball. This is particularly true on the long snaps for punts and field goals. "They can really tee off on you then, when you've got your head down between your legs," says Mick. "We have to get a little help from our guards. They kind of protect me. They get close to me and if somebody's hovering over me they'll help out. But you still get rapped pretty hard. You have to be mentally tough and not worry about getting hit, because if you think about it, it might affect your snap. My number one job is getting the ball back as fast as I can to the holder or the punter.

"I don't even worry about blocking too much because I've got my head down between my legs. I've also got two backs right behind me who, hopefully, will pick up anyone who breaks through. If a man just wants to punish me, that's okay because he's not going to block the kick. If he wants to block it, he's going to have to try to go around me, not bury me."

On punts, Tingelhoff tries to center the ball right back into the kicker's numbers. On field goals, he tries to get the ball back with the laces forward so the holder doesn't have to take the time to turn the ball around. If the center works on it, it's not as impossible as it may sound.

"If you're exactly seven yards away and you hold the ball the same way and snap it the same way every time," says Mick, "it should go back the same way every time. I've had very good success with this. Earlier this year in an exhibition game I snapped one where the laces were back. So the next day in practice I worked on it and found that I had to turn the ball one half a turn before I snapped it. Since then they've all gone back with the laces forward. I don't know if other centers worry about this, but I think it's important to your field-goal kicking game."

All centers are definitely concerned about snapping the ball back to the quarterback so that the laces are up on the fingertips of his right hand. The quarterback shouldn't have to rotate the ball when he's dropping back to pass. There just isn't time for that.

"Most of the quarterbacks I've played with also want the ball snapped to them hard—good and firm," says Mick. "All of them hold their hands a little differently so it's something you have to work out together. But it's a center's responsibility to get the ball back any way the quarterback wants it, so the center has to adjust. I don't know exactly how much we snap every day in practice, but I'd imagine it's a couple of hundred times. After a while you naturally get to know the quarterback pretty well, and the snap becomes almost automatic.

"A center can snap either with one hand or with two hands. It really doesn't make that much difference. Sometimes I snap with one, sometimes with two. When I snap with two, the left hand is just resting on the ball. The reason I sometimes snap with two hands is that it gets me lower and it gets my shoulders level. You like to keep your shoulders level so that you're balanced."

It is ironic but Mick Tingelhoff came into pro football as an unknown free agent from Nebraska in 1962. Even after making All-Pro five straight times, he's still often unknown and unnoticed. It is the nature of the position he plays. Who watches the center knocking down on the middle linebacker or picking up a blitzer?

"This doesn't bother me except for one thing I've noticed in the papers," Tingelhoff says. "If we lose a ballgame I often read that it was because the offensive line didn't give the quarterback protection. But if we win a ballgame it's because the quarterback hit 15 of 20 passes and all the backs ran for 100 yards." He shrugs. "They don't notice us until we lose, and then we're to blame."

Specialists

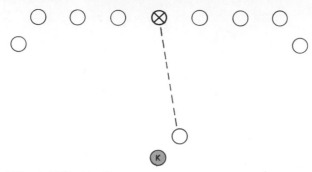

JIM BAKKEN
Place-Kicker

Jim Bakken is an atypical pro football player. He does not have to have size or speed or an overwhelming desire to hit people. In fact, he stands six feet tall and weighs just 200 pounds. He doesn't have to play very much—seldom more than 30 seconds per ballgame. Yet he decides the outcome of more games than any other single player on the field except the quarterback. He is the place-kicker.

Bakken doesn't have the speed to be a regular receiver in the National Football League. But he is one of the best place-kickers in professional football. He started kicking field goals in high school at Madison, Wisconsin, and continued his specialty at the University of Wisconsin. From there he was drafted by the Los Angeles Rams in 1962. Released, he joined the St. Louis Cardinals and promptly began an extra-point kicking streak that reached 124 before he finally missed one.

During his third season in the League, Bakken admitted that someday he would like to break the NFL record of five field goals in a game. Two years later Garo Yepremian, the soccer-style kicker who was then with the Detroit Lions, actually did break the record by kicking six in a game. In 1967 Jim Bakken topped Yepremian. He kicked *seven* field goals against the Pittsburgh Steelers. He would have had eight on an easy 23-yarder, if he hadn't looked up to watch the flight of the ball.

"The temptation was strong to look up as soon as I connected with the ball on that seventh kick," Bakken says. "But I resisted it. Golf taught me the importance of keeping the

head down. I learned that anyone who looks up too quickly to see where the ball is going won't like what he sees. On what should have been field goal number eight, I was too excited. I wanted so badly to see if it was good that I violated one of the basic rules of kicking."

There are not a lot of basic rules in place-kicking, but each of the fundamentals must be followed precisely if the ball is to twirl through the uprights. The mechanics are thoroughly mapped out.

"It's a two-step approach to the ball both on field goals and on extra points," Jim says. "A right-footed kicker would have his right foot slightly forward and the first step is with the right foot. The next step is a longer one with your left foot, and the left foot is placed about six inches back from the ball and is slightly to the left of the ball. Then there's the follow-through into the ball, emphasizing a good, high follow-through with the head down.

"Basically the extra point and the field goal are kicked the same way. But after a while you have a tendency—at least I do —to shorten up your steps a little bit on the shorter kicks. The thinking here is that you don't need the distance so much as the direction. On the extra points the main concern is making sure that you get the ball up in a hurry, trying to keep it out of the reach of the oncoming linemen. They seem to get bigger and bigger every year and they don't need a lot of penetration to get a hand on the ball if you don't get it up quick. You're not very much concerned about direction because it's such a short attempt. You just want to get it up fast."

Bakken is virtually impeccable on point-after-touchdown kicks. In fact, during his first pro kicking streak he actually kicked his 125th in succession in the game against the Browns. But an offside penalty forced him to have to kick over. That time Bakken's head came up too soon, his foot didn't hit the ball squarely, and the referee signaled that the P-A-T had sailed wide.

Bakken says that more than 50 percent of a kicker's success is dependent on his mental attitude under pressure. Staying cool and relaxed is even more important than concentrating on the fundamentals, because the fundamentals should become automatic after a while. Besides, no matter how much a kicker concentrates on his job, he's still never absolutely sure how accurate he'll be.

"I can never really tell from practicing before a game whether I'll do well that day," Jim says. "I've had some bad days in practice and then done well in the game. And I've had some very good days in practice and then done badly in the game. I don't use the pre-game warm-up drill as a barometer.

"What I like to do when I go out on the field in warm-ups is to use that time to make sure I've got the fundamentals down. I get on the field before a game and reaffirm in my mind that I have the fundamentals down. For example, my steps, my follow-through, my contact with the ball—in other words, hitting the ball solid—and getting good height on the ball. Generally you can tell if you're doing something wrong. It gets kind of fine, but if the ball slides a little bit to the right, you have an idea that you may not have had your ankle locked properly on contact. If you hit the ball too high, you may be too far back from the ball. If you hit the ball too low, you might be crowding it too much, kicking it from in too close."

Jim Turner of the New York Jets, who is one of the best place-kickers in the game, maintains that the man who holds the ball "is 70 percent of the place-kicking game. He's got to get the ball down there in the right spot every time, laces forward. And all the while he's got to be exuding confidence for the benefit of the kicker. The whole thing has got to be smooth and confident."

"Some kickers will say that the holder is as much as 75 percent of the kicking game," says Bakken. "But I rate all three men involved about the same. I think the center is one-third of it, the holder is one-third, and the kicker is one-third of it. But on some kicks the center's percentage can go down and the holder's can go up. For instance, if the center snap is poor, then the center's third of the overall efficiency goes down. But the holder can make up for it if he makes a nice recovery and gets the ball down fast enough."

After joining the Cardinals, Bakken had a regular holder—free safety Larry Wilson—and a backup holder—flanker

Bobby Joe Conrad—until the 1969 season. Then Conrad went to the Dallas Cowboys. "Bobby, who used to be a field-goal kicker himself, did a remarkably good job whenever Larry wasn't available," says Jim. "As long as he was with us I really didn't worry too much when the regular holder was side-lined."

The first thing Bakken does when he goes out on the field before a ballgame is check the wind. He tries to gauge the velocity and direction from which it is blowing. In some stadiums, the wind blows from several directions.

"Cleveland can be particularly difficult because it's right on Lake Erie and the stadium's a horseshoe," Bakken says. "So the wind comes in the same end that it goes out. It swirls right around. You can really be kicking against the wind both ways.

"But I think Yankee Stadium is about the toughest to kick in because of the wind conditions. St. Louis usually plays the Giants near the end of the season when the weather's cold and there's more wind." If it's simply a cross wind, Bakken can compensate, as he did in San Francisco a few years ago. Though there is often a strong wind at Kezar Stadium, too, in this particular game it was blowing steadily straight across the field. So Jim, kicking from the 35-yard line, aimed his kick ten yards to the right side of the upright. "I hooked it in just like a good iron shot to the green."

Bakken doesn't regard any one team as being more difficult to kick against than another. "A few years ago," he says, "Philadelphia would give me a tough time because they had a couple of men on the outside who used to rush very well. So I had to get the kick off a little faster. Over the years I'd say Dallas has put as much pressure on a field-goal attempt as anyone else. But I try not to worry about the rush at all, just concentrate on kicking."

Although many place-kickers feel that the shorter kicks coming from extreme angles are even tougher than the 40-yarders, Bakken finds the opposite is true for him. "Because there are so many things that come into play—the wind, the distance, the playing conditions—kicking the long ball is very difficult. The longer the kick, the more time the wind has to change the ball's course. The 15-yarder from any place on the field, hash mark to hash mark, should be automatic, though I've missed some of them too.

"But playing conditions—for instance, a muddy or wet field —can also cause a lot of trouble. On a muddy field there's the possibility of my slipping as I approach the ball, or even as I kick. And when the ball's set down in the mud it doesn't always come out of there as well. Though they wipe it off, the ball soaks up a certain amount of water and this makes it difficult to get off a good strong kick into the ball."

The toughest kick Bakken ever had to try came on a dry field in St. Louis in 1967. The Cardinals were tied with Dallas and there were ten seconds left to play when Jim trotted onto the field to attempt a 43-yarder that would win the game. "I didn't make it," Jim says. "The ball slid just a little bit to the right." It was one of those that would have gone through the uprights from the 20 or possibly even the 30. But from out at the 43 it had too far to travel.

"Another tough one that I did make was against Philadelphia in about 1966," he says. "We were behind by two points with about five seconds left on the clock and we tried a field goal from the 32 and made it. But the officials called a penalty and I had to kick again. Actually, I thought the penalty was against the Cardinals. But it was against the Eagles. They were penalized before the play got under way, so the official said the ball was dead. We had to kick it all over again. We would just as soon have declined the penalty, of course. But we tried it again from five yards closer and made it again, so we won the game."

Like most place-kickers, Bakken also kicks off for the Cardinals. The secret here is preparation, practice and timing. "You have to make sure that your approach to the ball isn't too fast or too slow," Jim says. "And when you reach the ball you have to have the proper timing with your leg swing and your momentum. You can work this out on the practice field by yourself. I've seen big kickers overpower the ball and I've seen smaller kickers have just about the same effect because they have tremendous timing."

Against certain outstanding kick returners, such as Gale Sayers of the Bears, Bakken tries to place his kickoffs. "When you're facing a guy who has that kind of tremendous speed, you may want to keep the ball away from him if you can. We discuss it. This is part of your game plan, your kicking game. I guess it's almost as important as your offensive or defensive game plan. You spend time on it, discussing the people who are returning the ball, discussing the different returns they've been using. If we have to face a guy like Sayers, we'll go over it before we kick off and say, I'm gonna get it down in the right or left corner.

"But by and large, we have speedy enough guys on the kickoff team so that a ball kicked nice and high and landing on the goal line can get good coverage. I'm a safety on the kickoff and I go down to about the 35-yard line and veer myself on the ball carrier. The object of the safetyman is to get out in front of the ball carrier when he breaks out of the initial pack so that he doesn't get too much of a head start. I haven't made a whole lot of tackles over the years. In the 1969 preseason, I guess I made as many tackles as I made in all of 1968. We were having some problems on our coverage then. But we did have success kicking the ball down into the corner against Chicago and Kansas City in preseason games, so a little preparation and planning has worked on occasions."

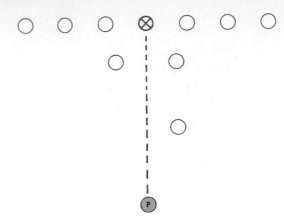

BILLY LOTHRIDGE
Punter

As a quarterback for the Georgia Tech football team, Billy Lothridge couldn't handle the ball very sharply, run very fast or pass with the quickness and strength of a potential pro. But he set 13 all-time records at Tech, tied another and was the school's only player ever to gain more than 1,000 yards total offense (passing and running) in a single season. Lothridge piled up 1,484 yards in 1962 and 1,240 yards the following season. In the 1963 Heisman Trophy voting, Billy Lothridge finished second to Roger Staubach of the Naval Academy.

Still, Lothridge knew full well he would never be a passer in pro football. "I knew I wasn't going to be a quarterback when I reported to the Cowboys," says Lothridge. "I knew I'd have to make it kicking, or I'd have to make my living another way."

Dallas drafted him in the sixth round in 1964 because the Cowboys needed a kicker to replace Sam Baker, whom they had just traded to Philadelphia for receiver Tommy McDonald. Lothridge had excellent kicking credentials. He had averaged 41 yards per punt on 46 attempts as a collegian, and he had booted a National Collegiate Athletic Association record 21 field goals.

As a Cowboy rookie, Lothridge kicked the longest punt of the NFL season—a 75-yarder against San Francisco. But he is not a super-long kicker. He is a guy who kicks the ball high,

hanging it up there for as long as possible to allow his coverage men to get down and prevent a return. This is what the
Cowboys were looking for. Although Sam Baker had always
been a long kicker, too many of his punts tended to be
returned. In 1963 only 13 of Baker's 49 punts were not re-

turned. During the 1964 exhibition season, Cowboy coach Ermal Allen said, "From the time the ball is snapped until it's caught or hits the ground, Lothridge averages 7.4 seconds. Baker used to average six seconds. Lothridge keeps the ball *in the air* for six seconds. Baker keeps it there for five." That extra second is the difference between a fair catch and a return. In other words, you are better off sacrificing a few yards in distance if you are fairly certain the ball cannot be run back. There is no percentage in averaging 45 yards per kick if each of them is returned ten yards. A 40-yard kick with no return is five yards better.

Lothridge averaged 40.3 yards per punt in 1964, but his problem was inconsistency. He almost always kicked very high and he occasionally boomed 60- and 70-yarders, but too often he also nubbed 30-yarders. At the season's end, the Cowboys traded him to the Baltimore Colts, where he showed flashes of brilliance along with chunks of inconsistency. He was released during the exhibition season and caught on with the Rams. Again he was inconsistent, averaging 38.5 yards per punt through nine games. Released, Lothridge thought his pro career was over until the NFL expanded to Atlanta. He signed with the Falcons in 1966. Back at the scene of his college heroics, Billy Lothridge finally found consistency.

"I really can't say exactly how it happened," says Billy. "But when I came to Atlanta Hal Herring, who was the defensive coach, helped me quite a bit with my kicking. We worked on the development of techniques and doing the same thing every time. We just went over it and over it and over it . . . and finally it just kind of all meshed together.

"The basic mechanics are just the steps and the drop. I usually set up about 14 yards behind the line and I normally take three steps on every punt—move left, right, left and kick. But if the ball is on, say, our own one-yard line, and I'm only lined up about ten yards behind the line, I'll take only two steps. But I won't punt any differently otherwise. Everything is exactly the same.

"Now, on the drop, I drop the ball from just above waist high and I always try to keep the laces up. When you're kicking into a strong wind, you want to drop the ball a little lower and kick the ball a little lower, on a lower trajectory. You don't want to kick the ball up into the wind because it'll be held up and you won't get any distance. With the wind to my back, I just try to kick the ball regularly unless I'm trying to place the ball down near the goal line or aim for a certain spot."

Lothridge doesn't try to aim his punts away from outstanding return men, such as Gale Sayers of the Bears or Travis Williams of the Packers. "We don't set up anything in particular," he says. "The main thing is to get height. Height is just as important as distance in punting. You've got guys standing back there with 9.5 or 9.6 speed, so you want to kick the ball nice and high so that your coverage men will have the time to get down and cover it. The other teams always set up which way their return will go—right, left or up the middle. Every team has a return set up on every kick, and you have to be prepared to stop it. We go over this with our special teams all the time in preparing for a game. We see in the films which way our opponent tends to return and we get ready for it. This is a very intricate part of the game and we go over it two or three times in practice every week.

"The thing is, most teams just naturally try to return to the wide side of the field, where they'll have the most running room. Generally we just try to kick the ball straight away and to cover straight away with every man coming down in his lane. We might converge toward the wide side of the field at times. That would be the only specific thing we'd do or plan. Now I'm a safetyman on punts. So after the kick is away I always go to the left side. The fullback, who is back blocking for me, always goes to the right side. That way we're covered on both sides in the deep middle."

Lothridge gets the ball off quickly and he has been fortunate in that he's always played with teams that block well on punts. As a result, in his first six years as a pro, he had only two kicks blocked.

"I've had pretty good luck," Billy says. "I had one blocked during my rookie year, and Minnesota blocked one on me in 1965 when I was with the Rams. But I try not to be aware of the rush that much. I just try to concentrate on getting the kick off. My main purpose is to kick the ball. And it's someone else's job to keep them [the rush men] out of there.

"I don't think there are any teams that are tougher to kick against than others, though some people seem to think so. I guess Los Angeles tries to block more punts than anyone else. Against someone like that, I'd probably be rushed a little more, personally, as far as taking my steps. I guess it would affect me more mentally than anything else. But, as I said, I try not to be aware of the rush, and when we're going up against a team like Los Angeles we always work a little harder to get the ball off quickly. The Rams have never blocked one on me."

A lot of punters hate to play in certain stadiums because of the way the winds swirl around, sending kicked footballs on weird arcs. Yankee Stadium, where the New York Giants play, is such a place late in the season. Yet Lothridge says, "I don't have much of a problem there. I've kicked at the stadium at least twice and I've always done well. But the wind factor can be a problem in an open-end stadium, in contrast to a closed or a domed type of stadium like ours here in Atlanta. San Francisco, for example, is always a hard place to kick in. The wind is always blowing there and you never know exactly what it's going to do at a particular time."

Lothridge, who stands six feet one and weighs 195 pounds, says there is no such thing as a set of physical requirements for a punter. "I don't think size has anything to do with making a successful punter, really. David Lee of the Baltimore Colts weighs 230 pounds, about 35 more than I do. There are a lot of punters who are smallish and get results. This is especially true if you look at some of the place kickers.

"I think the timing and the drop of the ball are more important than anything else in punting. It's just like playing golf. You know that if the rhythm is there and everything, you can punt the ball. That's why I work on my timing every day. I kick every day. Before practice, I kick maybe 20 or 25 times. If I'm kicking well, I won't kick as much. If I'm kicking bad, I'll try to kick a little bit more. I can usually tell what's going wrong when I'm kicking bad. One of the coaches is usually standing by, and he can spot something. Coach Norm Van Brocklin was a punter, you know, and he will say, 'You're dropping the ball bad,' or 'You're taking too long a step' or whatever. As I said, you can tell yourself but it's good to have another opinion you respect. Then you go back and work on whatever it is you're doing wrong. Once you get back in the groove you know it, and you can relax."

Lothridge has relaxed since he joined the Falcons, particularly after the 1967 season when he led the National Football League in punting with a 43.7-yards-per-kick average.

Although he's not a fast runner, Billy is shifty, and he has picked up a number of important first downs over the years by running with the ball instead of punting.

"I never go into a punting situation with my mind made up to run," he says. "Occasionally we plan a pass play in a punting situation, but if one of the linemen blocks too far down-field he becomes an ineligible receiver and I have to run."

This was the case some years ago against Minnesota. Back to kick from his own 34-yard line in a fourth-and-nine situation, Billy saw the Viking rush men drop back to block for a return. He also saw an aggressive Falcon lineman blocking down-field, which made the lineman an ineligible receiver and killed the pass play. So Lothridge tucked the ball under his arm and zigged 16 yards for the first down. Falcon quarterback Randy Johnson then took the team in for a touchdown and a lead Atlanta never lost in a 21-20 victory.

"When I run," says Billy Lothridge, "I run because I see an open invitation to run, no rush and plenty of open field."

131

Of course, anytime a punter runs with the football instead of kicking it—without specific orders from his coach—the punter had better be very very certain he picks up the first down. Otherwise, when he runs off the field after the play, he might be safer running to the opposing sideline.

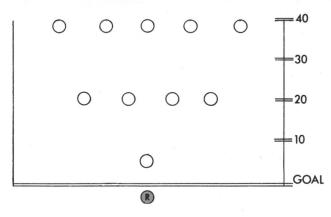

GALE SAYERS
Kick Returner

During his first season in the National Football League, Gale Sayers of the Chicago Bears proved to be such a devastating returner of kickoffs that opposing teams quickly took to booting the ball away from him. The following season the Bears countered by having Sayers and his return partner line up one behind the other under the goal posts so that the ball could not be kicked away from Gale. By the end of his third pro season, however, Sayers had already run back six kickoffs for touchdowns. That tied him with Ollie Matson for the all-time NFL career record for touchdown runs on kickoff returns. Of course, Matson compiled his record in 14 seasons. If Sayers plays that long, there's no telling what his total may reach.

The prospect worried some opposing coaches so much that they came up with a new gimmick to stop Sayers—kicking the ball so short that he couldn't return it. In other words, kicking it to the blockers. Giving up field position, they reasoned, wasn't as bad as giving up six points.

Sayers felt this was foolish, and said so at a luncheon a couple of years ago while the experiment was in full bloom. Giant quarterback Fran Tarkenton, who was at the luncheon along with several other players, agreed that it was much easier on the offense to get the ball upfield instead of down near its goal

133

line. "If you make a mistake inside the 20 you're in real trouble," said Fran. "Anything can kill you there. If you start on the 40 you can open up your game and go."

Fran paused, perhaps thinking of the 103-yard return Sayers had made on the opening kickoff of the season against Pittsburgh, or the 97 yards he had run with a kickoff to score against Detroit a couple of weeks later. "You have to remember," he added, "even when you get the ball on your 40, you still have 60 yards to go."

"I don't know," Sayers replied. "Green Bay kicked short to us. We got the ball on the 40 once and went to a touchdown. We lost, 13-10, but it was pretty close."

Tarkenton's face split in a wide grin.

"The Rams didn't kick to me either," Sayers continued. "They were short and we scored off one of them."

"Who won the game?" asked Fran.

"L.A. did, 28-17," Gale said.

"The prosecution rests," said Tarkenton, sitting down.

What does it take to make a great kick returner like Gale Sayers? Mostly it takes a great runner, a man with excellent speed and the ability to accelerate instantly. His moves should be instinctive, coupled with a style of cutting—on his heels in Sayers' case—that allows him to make sharper, quicker changes of direction than anyone else can. But beyond all this the job takes knowledge and experience . . . and guts.

"I would say almost anyone, no matter how he's built, can run back kickoffs if he has the intestinal fortitude," says Sayers. "Courage is probably the main requirement, because you can get hit pretty hard. I remember one time in my rookie year when I got clotheslined by Wally Hilgenberg [the linebacker who was with Detroit then]. It almost took my head off. (In a "clothesline" a defender sticks his arm straight out at Adam's-apple level and lets a runner race into it. This naturally tends to stop the runner rather abruptly.)

"I mean, you really can get hurt," Gale continues. "Heck,

Stone Johnson of the Kansas City Chiefs got killed on a
kickoff team in 1965. These fellows are coming down on you
at 90 miles an hour. If you don't see the whole field, you can
really get smashed. It's when you get hit blind that you can
really get wiped out.

"That's why I try to take in the whole field, so I can see where all the defensive guys are. But I think I have pretty good peripheral vision. Actually, this is why I think returning kicks is the easiest part of football. Because you can see the men coming down at you, the whole field's in front of you. It's not like being at the line of scrimmage, where you have a limited area in which to operate. Say you run the end; you only have about ten yards before you hit the sidelines. Returning kicks you have from one sideline to the other to run in."

When Gale is on the field most teams kicking off to the Bears hope to put the ball out of the end zone. But Sayers still has to line up under the goal post with his return partner standing right in front of him in order to prevent teams from aiming the ball away from him. As the kicker starts running to kick off, Sayers yells "Right" or "Left," which is the side his partner is to cover. Gale has a pretty good idea where the ball will go because he knows all the kickers and he checks the kickoff tee location as he trots onto the field.

"That's the first thing you have to know," says Sayers. "Where the ball is being kicked from. Some teams kick it from one hash mark, others kick it from the middle of the field, and some kick it from the other hash mark. In each case the ball's line of flight is different. If the kick is from the hash mark, you have to adjust your position. One man would cover from the hash mark to the out-of-bounds, while the other would move over to the middle to handle everything else.

"Now, when the ball is on the way, the most important thing to do is keep your eye on it. All kickoff and punt returners have that urge to look upfield to see how close the defense is. But you can't do that until you've caught the ball, or you'll misjudge it and maybe miss it entirely."

Like every pro football team, the Bears carefully study films of each opponent, looking for a weakness in the team's kick coverage. The men who run down to stop the kickoff returner —and the punt returner as well—race down in lanes. Each man has an area five yards wide for which he is responsible.

Usually films reveal one or two men who tend to loaf a bit while getting downfield, or perhaps a rookie who is so anxious to get into the play that he leaves his area unprotected too soon. These "weak" lanes are the ones the kick returners aim at when they call a right, left or middle return before the kick. Of course, the way the ball is kicked—say, to the opposite side of the call—often determines the return route, too. As does the way the blocks are thrown.

"The blockers are the key," says Sayers. "There are five men up front and then the four-man wedge about 20 yards ahead of you and the other returner. The wedge men and the return men have to work out between them when the wedge is going to take off after the catch. With the Bears, when I get ten yards from the wedge, it takes off. The captain of the wedge is Dick Butkus. He judges when I'm close enough and tells them to take off. The return man who doesn't catch the kick takes the first defensive man downfield. Usually it's one of the fast outside men who try to come at you from the side.

"Then I just try to follow the wedge upfield. I run at what I like to call 'full speed under control.' I think I'm running between seven-eighths and full speed, but I can still make my cuts under control. I can still make my moves."

Sayers heads straight upfield behind the wedge, even when the call is a right or left return. The idea is to draw all the defenders into the center of the field before breaking off to one side or the other. On the middle return, blockers up front cross-block to create an open channel. This is the easiest return to score on because once the runner is past the wave of would-be tacklers, there is no one else to beat except the kicker, who acts as the safetyman.

"Once you break off your wedge block, there's nothing fancy to do until you get to the safetyman," says Sayers. "You just run the ball and hope everybody on the kickoff team makes his block. You hit the opening and turn on the speed. If it gets jammed up, sometimes you can cut back across the grain of your pursuit. This usually occurs on a left or right return. If you reach the clear except for the safetyman, who keeps dropping back to protect against the touchdown, you usually have to put only one or two moves on him."

Gale Sayers remembers the final score of ballgames better than he remembers the big kickoff returns he has made in the NFL. Only one return really stands out in his mind. "We needed it to win the ballgame," he says simply.

It occurred during his rookie season, 1965, and was one of the 22 touchdowns—a league record—he scored that year. There were less than two minutes to go in the game when the Minnesota Vikings scored, moving ahead by six points. The Vikings were still congratulating themselves on the sideline when the kickoff sailed downfield and settled in the arms of Sayers. He ran straight up the middle, hesitated a split second as the wedge chopped a hole at the 20-yard line. Then he accelerated through the gap, cut to his left as a tackler flew past him, swung back to his right at the 40 to get past another man and raced into the end zone. Ninety-seven yards without being touched. The Viking self-congratulations ended very abruptly.

"Punt returning is probably a little more dangerous than kickoff returning," Sayers says, "because you never can tell exactly how close they are to you when you catch the ball. You have to concentrate on the ball in the air and by the time you catch a punt they're usually on you. On a kickoff you're usually running before they hit you and you see them coming.

"As far as the actual running goes, it's no different from the kickoff return except that on a punt you have to make your move right away. If you can slip that first wave of tacklers, well, you should have a pretty good return. The kicker is the only man they keep back as a rule, and he's usually no speed demon. Donny Anderson, who kicks for Green Bay, and Lem Barney, who does some punting for the Lions, are fast, but there aren't many like them."

Many teams, including the Bears, are now using their super returner as a single deep safety, with another returner some ten yards in front of him to handle short punts. Sayers, who is captain of the Bear punt-return team, positions himself roughly ten yards beyond the punter's average kick. That is, if the punter averages 45 yards (from the line of scrimmage) per kick, Gale drops back some 55 yards from the line of scrimmage. The short man waits 45 yards from the line of scrimmage and, if the kick is to him, listens for Sayers to tell him what to do.

"If the defense is coming down real fast, I will yell for him to make a fair catch," says Gale. "Otherwise I run up and try to block the first man down on him. If the ball comes to me, it's his responsibility to take the first man down. I can usually judge whether or not to call a fair catch for myself, so he doesn't have that job. I'm ten yards deeper and have a bit more time. If the punter kicks it very high, it usually doesn't go 45 yards and you can't return those most of the time. If the punt goes 45 yards, it's usually more of a line drive, which means I can return it."

As with the kickoff return, the call is made beforehand—left, right or middle. Again, the call is determined by any weakness discovered in films. Somebody is not doing his job properly, not guarding his lane. "If it's a left or right return, a wall of blockers forms to the side you're running," says Sayers. "Your men hit and try to contain their men at the line just long enough for you to have some running room when you get the ball."

This wall or picket line that is so often seen on television is not formed by magic or by players running in off the bench. The linemen may rush the kicker, then turn and peel back along one sideline. Or, more likely, on a return aimed not at blocking the punt but at picking up yardage on a runback, the linemen hit their opponents for a count of two or three. They try to keep them from getting down to the return man too fast, then wheel around and run back along the sideline to set up the wall.

Meanwhile, the returner, Sayers, usually runs up the middle after he's gotten past the first tackler. This draws all the pursuit into the center of the field. When Sayers then cuts toward the sideline where the wall has been erected, the pursuit dashes right into it. Gale races along the chalk and hopes the wall holds. Of course, if he sees it crumbling up ahead, he can always break off on a diagonal back inside. The main thing is to beat that first tackler and then get behind the wall. If he does those two things he won't necessarily go for a touchdown every time out, but he will have picked up good yardage for a punt return. Remember, a 12- to 15-yard average leads the league most seasons. On kickoff returns, the leader often averages over 30 yards.

Punts are not returned for touchdowns as often as kickoffs, but Sayers has had more than his share already, as the San Francisco 49ers will readily attest. "I've had good success against them," says Sayers. "In my rookie year we played them on a muddy field, and I always seem to do well in the mud." (He cuts on his heels and thus keeps his traction while tacklers are slipping and sliding.) "I took a low line-drive kick on the run, cut to my right, made a quick move and got by the first wave of tacklers. The tacklers started chasing me upfield, but they ran into my blockers coming back downfield to set up the wall. I remember Ken Willard was chasing me from behind and, as I cut back to the left against the grain to avoid some men, he got a hand on my leg. But I made a little move and pulled away. I went about 85 yards for a touchdown."

Two years later, in 1967, Sayers returned only three punts all season (he called for eight fair catches). Unfortunately for the 49ers, one of those punt returns came against them. "It was kind of a high kick," Sayers recalls, "and I really felt I caught them a little by surprise when I returned it. I'm sure they felt I was going to call for a fair catch. But I took the kick, made a move and that was it. No one touched me. Steve Spurrier, who kicked the ball, was waiting for me at about the ten-yard line. But I made a quick move, cut by him and went into the end zone." It was a 58-yard touchdown.

"On a high punt, when they think you're calling for a fair

catch, you can sometimes catch them napping. They can't hit you until you touch the ball, so sometimes they start to slow up ten yards away, expecting you to put your arm up for a fair catch. When that happens, you can catch them flatfooted. Of course, sometimes it can be a little dangerous if they're not fooled, because they can hit you just as you catch the ball. And they're moving pretty fast."

It can hurt, all right. But you can be hurt worse when you have Gale Sayers returning kicks against you.

INDEX